I0606416

Praise for

GROW OR FOLD

"Matt Ross proves it's never too late to change everything. *Grow or Fold* is raw, honest, and packed with the kind of wisdom you only earn by living it. If you're at a crossroads in your life, this book will show you how to move forward on *your* terms."

MEL ROBBINS, *New York Times* bestselling author of *The Let Them Theory* and host of *The Mel Robbins Podcast*

"Matt Ross has done a remarkable job staring life's greatest challenges in the eye and moving through them thoughtfully and with great passion. Midlife is such a unique time for all of us and a chance to reset our path for the rest of our lives, and Matt's journey and compelling toolkit will light a fire in you and help guide you through the process of transforming your life."

JACK CANFIELD, coauthor of the #1 *New York Times* bestselling Chicken Soup for the Soul® series and *The Success Principles™: How to Get from Where You Are to Where You Want to Be*

"*Grow or Fold* is a wake-up call for anyone who thinks midlife is about coasting. Matt Ross takes you inside the messiness of reinvention with grit, humor, and hard-won wisdom from a life in music, art, and business. He shows that midlife isn't about slowing down—it's about choosing growth, even when the world dares you to fold."

MARSHALL GOLDSMITH, #1 *New York Times* bestselling author of *Triggers, What Got You Here Won't Get You There,* and *The Earned Life*

MATTROSS.COM

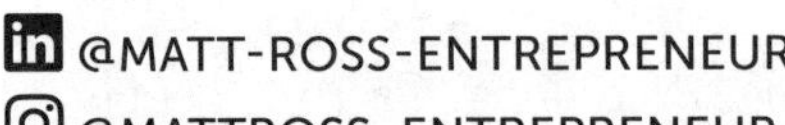

www.amplifypublishinggroup.com

Grow or Fold: Transform Yourself in Midlife and Beyond

For more information, please contact:
Amplify Publishing, an imprint of Amplify Publishing Group
620 Herndon Parkway, Suite 220
Herndon, VA 20170
info@amplifypublishing.com

Library of Congress Control Number: 2025915613

CPSIA Code: PRV0925A

ISBN-13: 979-8-89138-865-9

Printed in the United States

GROW OR FOLD

Transform Yourself *in* Midlife *and* Beyond

MATT ROSS

Life Lessons *from a* Creative Entrepreneur

CONTENTS

PART II: GROW OR FOLD

PART III: THE POWER OF PURE GROWTH

INTRODUCTION

One day I had an idea—I should write a book. It happened during a moment of self-reflection and, to be frank, a moment of accomplishment. For the first time in my life, I truly felt at peace, and that was when the idea of documenting my journey popped into my head. As I sat in my kitchen in 2018, I found myself thinking two things:

1. During the previous decade, middle age had presented such overwhelming challenges.
2. Somehow, I summoned a new mindset and the strength to tackle these challenges.

And I felt compelled to share my story to help others. That is how this book was born.

The work began when I turned fifty and figured out what was missing in my life. After thirty years of building businesses, navigating ups and downs, and engaging in advanced education, courses, coaches, books, tapes, and programs, I embarked on a rigorous exploration of how to tackle the challenges of midlife and ensure I was prepared to be happy, healthy, and prosperous.

Today, I'm certain that because of the work I did, I have activated the kind of future that I always wanted, deserved, and had access to. This book allows me to share my stories and the toolkit I built from the ground up, which was created to help others drive personal and professional transformation in midlife and beyond.

GROW OR FOLD

Grow or Fold is a simple metaphor I created to describe the pivotal moments that govern the arc of our lives: *We are either growing or folding.*

But, unlike a flower that begins to decay and move toward an inevitable ending, our lives can continue to change and grow profoundly as we age. But it requires us to spend our time doing the things that drive progress while also investing in ways to evolve our thinking and behavior. Scientists used to believe that our brains stopped growing at twenty years old and began a slow decline from there. How depressing! How wrong! Today, it is well understood that we can create new brain matter and improve processing well into our later years. So how do we continue to grow, learn, change, reset our priorities, and redefine our future?

My story is one of trial and error and not unlike most people's. But my transformation wasn't an accident. In the middle of my life, while dealing with catastrophic personal and professional challenges, I took the time to revisit everything I stood for. This painful experience allowed me to envision the future I wanted to achieve and identify the risks and sacrifices I would make to get there. For the previous thirty years, I had been hard at work developing unique personal and professional skills. Finally, at fifty, I had the courage and the foresight to deploy these skills in a more thoughtful and focused way to help me Grow rather than Fold. I firmly believe that everyone possesses a unique skill set that can be exploited to dramatically shift their future as well.

Within this book, I share a series of stories and present a condensed snapshot of my life to help explain the road I traveled leading to midlife. When you learn about the challenges I have dealt with, you may relate personally. This book is also written as a guide to help you identify the things that drive your core motivations in life and provides a process for developing a simple approach to spending more time doing the things you love to do and are best at. The potential for change and profound growth is universal—the architecture of the mind is virtually the same for all of us. We all thrive when fed the right things. In most cases, we can change our professional pathway and rewrite our personal journey. It starts with thinking and acting differently, with a healthy dose of creativity. Once you have discovered this and the pure benefits of activating it, you will be more at ease, happier, and healthier.

I hope my story, observations, and tools become a compelling resource that helps you reinvent how you live. When you hear about the time, effort, and work I put in and the ultimate success I have created for myself and my family, I hope you will understand more about how to make it happen for yourself.

Grow or Fold is a challenge that I now pass on to you.

If you want more during middle age and the rest of your life, join me in reading this book. Explore the tools I created. I am certain that change is simply a choice to **Grow or Fold.**

PART I

LET'S ROCK

Every great concert has a moment before the lights dim and the band hits the stage—a moment of anticipation, a deep breath before the first note rings out. That's where we are right now.

This book is about hitting life's middle years not with a whimper but with a roar. It's about standing at the crossroads of change—personally, professionally, emotionally—and choosing to rock your stage, no matter the setbacks, doubts, or challenges.

In this first section, you'll see how I wrestled with the big five-oh, that unavoidable milestone that forces all of us to ask, *Is this the beginning of my decline or a chance to grow?* You'll see how I navigated that frightening midlife inflection point, transforming personal hardships and career setbacks into a new vision for my future.

You'll meet my *creative soul*—the young boy fueled by music and performance. His early sparks of passion were nearly snuffed out, but he learned to fight for his creative identity later in life.

You'll come backstage with me as I build my professional competence, starting humbly but hustling hard, learning lessons in sales, leadership, resilience, and the absolute power of showing up fully for others.

You'll feel the impact of *catastrophic challenge*: the gut-wrenching moments that change everything—my son's diagnosis, life-threatening emergencies—the kind of events that could have broken me but instead fueled growth, resilience, and a deeper purpose.

You'll see how I found a calling with School of Rock that reconnected me to my creative roots, entrepreneurial spirit, and belief in building something bigger than myself. But with the highs came brutal challenges and new tests of faith and strength—proof that no matter how good you get at riding the waves, life always throws bigger ones at you.

Through it all, these early chapters set the foundation for everything that follows:

- taking personal responsibility,
- knowing yourself deeply,
- believing you can change,
- facing hard change head-on, and
- honoring the creative force within you.

It's easy to let fear and doubt get in the way of writing your song. But this book—and this moment—is your reminder that the music is still inside you. It's time to tune your instrument, find your band, step onto the stage, and play like your life depends on it. Because it does.

Let's rock.

CHAPTER ONE

THE BIG FIVE-OH

Midlife Crisis or Midlife Opportunity?

While I've never been one to have anxiety about getting older, turning *fifty* was different.

The big FIVE-OH!

For the first time in my life, aging became an obsessive area of focus, and I was starting to worry deeply about things that never seemed to bother me before. You would never know it from the outside, but on the inside, things were moving in a direction that I couldn't quite grasp. After working so hard to achieve so much, I started feeling lost and uncertain about how to create the future I wanted. I was overwhelmed and exhausted, and two dominant, conflicting questions rattled around my brain:

1. Was this the beginning of a downward spiral in health, productivity, mind, body, and spirit?
2. Was there something profoundly different that I could do to define and live the life that would bring me my greatest happiness?

The journey to get here was filled with many of the uncontrollable challenges that so many of us face: my child's profound disability and health issues, the changing tides of my career, familial dysfunction, and more. And now, as I was right in the center of middle age, it felt like I had lost control over everything. It is a scary feeling when, no matter where you look, you feel like you are the passenger on a turbulent roller coaster—and not one of those fun and quick coasters. It was a jerky and uncomfortable ride that would never end. Inevitably, though, after months of suffering through a nonstop mental loop, it came down to answering one fundamental question:

> Was I prepared to make fundamental changes to how I thought, behaved, and spent my time to galvanize my growth?

Something had to change. But was it me or the environmental factors around me? Eventually, I surrendered to the idea that the only thing I could control was how I responded to the challenges I faced.

I have always been fast moving and driven to succeed, with a deep connection to what my body and emotions were telling me—*at all times*. Yes, I have lived with the curse of constant inner thoughts swirling around my head while trying to navigate life, and, all too often, this *dual messaging* created a real *duel of challenges and emotions*. We usually live at the intersection of our problems and adversity. It can come from multiple directions simultaneously, and one version of your adversity doesn't check to see what the others are doing. When they collide, and they often do, it can feel like you face insurmountable challenges.

While this may sound familiar or seem like a curse, it can be a real blessing in many ways. For me, I navigated a career that led me into roles where my creative thinking and my ability to process numerous streams of information allowed me to build winning brand marketing and business strategies. My hyper intuition and active mind allowed me to lead people and build trust while they were relying on me to help them learn and grow. My sensitivity enabled me to develop deep relationships with my family, staff, and friends, which I cherish and derive much strength and joy from. And, as a parent, my curious brain has been put to the task, as I have had to work through some of the most tragic and monumental parental challenges one can face.

Having said that, I felt confronted with a new reality at fifty years old. Years ago, I read a business book by Marshall Goldsmith called *What Got You Here Won't Get You There*. The book told the story of how successful executives needed to make changes to stay successful, and for whatever reason, the book title was constantly popping into my head. Once I started to listen to the whispers, I realized it was also a metaphor that described where I was and the drastic change I needed to make to every aspect of my life.

> I needed to completely reinvent myself, which required examining everything I did and creating a recipe for how I would live over the next fifty years.

It was 2011, and the punches kept coming. We all deal with crises occasionally, but I was dealing with a giant mountain of issues, most of which I had no control over. My sixteen-year-old, nonverbal, and severely autistic son, Alex, had a complete psychiatric breakdown, and I was suddenly having health issues. My father and father-in-law were slowly dying. My mother and mother-in-law were declining. My two siblings were off the rails, stuck in addiction and depression, and one was flirting with suicide. Now what? After I engineered the sale of School of Rock, a company I built as CEO from an early-stage, struggling business into the leader in music education for kids, I was suddenly replaced.

In 2009, when we sold the company to a private equity firm, I knew that there was personal risk, but it was the right thing to do at the time to raise the capital we needed to drive growth. After the deal closed, I quickly realized I didn't love working for them. They were formulaic and overly involved in the hiring process, which drove me crazy. For instance, they thought, for some reason, that a bunch of guys from the fast-food space would be the right people to help me manage School of Rock. They were wrong and didn't understand our culture, people, and processes. After a year together, we agreed to part ways.

It is hard to imagine that all of this could happen at once, and as I evaluated my life in shambles, I remember asking myself two profound questions:

1. Was 2011 going to break me or become a significant turning point?
2. Would I Grow or Fold?

Somehow a switch went off for me, and I remember it like yesterday. *Grow or Fold* became my mantra because things were fragile, and there was no time to waste. No matter what happened in my personal life, I had to figure out my professional path. I also needed to provide leadership and financial stability for my family when everything was seemingly falling apart. While I received some cash when we sold School of Rock, I rolled all my equity into the business, and it was clear that my investment would be tied up for many years to come. As my severance began to run out, I started interviewing for jobs and was focused on the next phase of my professional life. However, no matter what interviews I had, I always left the meetings uneasy.

For the first time, I was profoundly aware that *I was in the heart of middle age and felt more vulnerable than ever before.* Still, amidst all the challenges I was dealing with, I had lots of energy and drive. My skills were refined, and I had great confidence in myself. When I reflected on my experience, I hated the idea of once again putting my heart and soul on the line for a company and not being able to control my destiny, especially at this stage of my life. Prior to leading School of Rock, during all my professional time in the media business, I had been at the mercy of corporate structures that ultimately allowed others to determine my fate. Even though I was a large investor in School of Rock, I didn't own or personally control the business, and this lack of control was par for the course in my thirties and forties. I couldn't stomach it anymore. I wanted to reset my professional goals to control the direction of my life and work with people I liked. I also wanted to invest my time in ways that allowed me to support a purpose that mattered.

Perhaps more importantly, I had to find peace in my personal life and calm the sense of fear and anxiety, which was in such a heightened state given all that I was navigating. *So, I leaned in on my proven professional skill set and entrepreneurial sensibility.* I started to think that this toolkit that helped me in business could also help me evolve past my challenges and reset my life. Over the years, I have developed many skills to help companies ideate on their challenges, goals, strategies, and tactics, but for some reason, I never applied the same tools to a thoughtful analysis of my life! I had the tools but wasn't using them. This made me wonder,

> Why don't we deploy our professional toolkits to support our personal life planning?

There are so many reasons, but I believe it comes down to this:

- We are generally unwilling to expose our actual weaknesses and challenges.
- It is hard to create the deep self-awareness and vulnerability that comes with it.
- In some cases, we may not possess the strategic skills or toolkit.
- It requires lots of time and effort to do this well.
- It is inherently problematic to do.

So, here's what humans—me included— do: We develop walls around our perspectives and rarely peel back the layers to revisit the core of who we are.

To that point, I decided to slow things down. I would never be fifty again and didn't want to regret that I hadn't built the right strategy for my life because I was too anxious about money and the ticking clock. So I chose to spend considerable time treating myself like a client, and the goal was to figure out a new personal and professional plan. I wanted to carefully look at how I lived my life, how I treated my body and mind, and how I allocated my time. So, now that you understand more about what I was experiencing, follow me into my basement.

Over the next few weeks, I tore myself apart and methodically made lists on top of lists. This old-fashioned brain dump became a once-in-a-lifetime chance to document what I wanted to do and was passionate about. Inevitably, I got large Post-its, tore out the two-foot by three-foot sheets, and covered my basement walls. This was, in essence, a creative brainstorming session; except this time, the brand was about *me* and not a marketing challenge. It was a life-planning assignment to understand what my true north looked like.

I used a basic diagram to help me sort through this. I first drew two axes and labeled the vertical axis "Love to Do" and the horizontal axis "Good At." Using this, I then created four boxes, or quadrants, and focused on the upper right box, where the holy grail resided. This box, labeled "Good At/Love to Do," listed all the traits and tasks that ultimately decided the work I should be doing for the rest of my life. However, I went deeper than just focusing on my best work attributes and most enjoyable tasks.

I conducted a separate analysis of my personal life, values, and goals, looking through a holistic lens that evaluated what drove me at my core. I was driven to reinvent myself and worked to create a career path that would yield the most happiness, not the most money. *At fifty years old, I took the time to deeply understand exactly what made me tick so that I could align my time, motivation, and commitment in the areas that best fit my profile.*

No matter your age, you can do the same. I want you to take a moment and do something similar. Remember, this specific exercise is focused on aligning your professional toolkit with your most excellent core competencies and the work that brings you joy. Grab a piece of paper and list what you love to do. Now, make a list of what you don't like doing. Grab another piece of paper and make a list of what you are great at and another list of your lesser competencies. You can return to this assignment as you think about what defines the work you should do to provide the most outstanding professional satisfaction.

I worked on this on and off during a two-month window and took time to sort through my traits, skills, motivations, and goals, which allowed me to become much more comfortable developing a plan to grow beyond where I was. It was a profound experience that I recommend everyone tackle during middle age. In the second part of this book, I will guide you through all the aspects of my workflow to help you.

The ups and downs of my career trajectory taught me that we often jump into our careers based on a notion of who we are when we are in our early twenties. Still, as we grow older and evolve into our true selves, we often get stuck in careers defined by who we were long ago. This also carries over to our personal lives—we develop hardwired habits. As a result, we often continue to do the *same things* the *same way*, even though we are unhappy, unhealthy, not growing, and frequently depressed, with no plans to change.

All too often, someone slams the door of growth, or we age out of a company or industry because the culture and demands have shifted and they are no longer aligned with our best selves. We get stuck in bad relationships, avoid taking great care of our bodies, and develop physical and mental health issues. The worst part is this: We rarely reflect on what's working, what's not working, and how to create change. So, as I was trying to consolidate all my analysis and was working toward refining a professional plan for myself, I couldn't get out of the way of a basic thought that took me twenty-five years to clarify as a straightforward fact: *I was good at building things and motivated to find another place to work that provided a similar chance to make a difference in people's lives.*

When I joined School of Rock at forty-five years old, it allowed me to tap into something I cared deeply about: helping kids develop their confidence through music education. As I started to think more and more about this, a new idea popped into my head:

What about building an art school?

This was a strange question for me to ask since I hadn't taken an art class since junior high school, and that was the only one I ever took. I had never taken an art history class!

I also knew very little about the art of today. Still, I developed a bit of curiosity and interest in learning more about it, fueled by a personal dynamic in my household. My younger son, Jason, and I share a deep sense of creative curiosity, and throughout his childhood, we visited art museums regularly. The museums of our current day are not like the museums of my childhood because now, rich media allows you to hear the curator or artist's voice and get an intimate perspective while learning the context and history behind the artist, their work, and their thinking. This immersive experience profoundly affected me, and I became turned on and motivated to learn more about contemporary art because of it.

In 2010, as this idea continued to percolate inside of my head, I visited the Whitney Biennial, a major survey of art that occurs every two years at the Whitney Museum in New York City. Strangely, I started to realize that, at the time, it seemed like no one really cared about the art of today in America. Compared to my reference points for culture, which were music, film, and television, there seemed to be a significant lack of top-of-mind awareness when it came to visual artists. This event at the Whitney was its seventy-fifth edition, and as I walked through each exhibit, I realized I hardly knew anything about the artists on display. If I knew only one artist, I was convinced that most people didn't know any! After talking about this with numerous family and friends, I was right—there just wasn't much broad awareness or national attention surrounding contemporary art.

After doing some research, I found out that there were over two million working artists in America. But for some reason, there was a giant chasm between the art of today and the public, who rarely had a chance to become exposed to, purchase, or engage in the most compelling contemporary art. The art world seemed to be the epitome of snobbery. I started to visit galleries throughout New York City, and almost every time I walked into a gallery, I felt like the experience was so unwelcoming. To make matters worse, all the "art speak" out there also turned me off. More questions popped into my head:

- Why wasn't the art world creating experiences to engage more people?
- Could I build an art school to teach art through the lens of living artists?
- Could I make learning art fun and help people grow?

Oh my god, I had so many thoughts. I was excited, but I was also going in a direction with little understanding of the subject matter. I spent the next two months thinking, reading, studying, and learning about contemporary art. I started researching recreational art schools throughout America and was deeply underwhelmed by what I found. So I decided to throw my whole body into it to learn more about the art of today and to see if I could respond to it in a personal and emotional way.

I went back to school. I signed up to take six courses at New York University's continuing education program, bought and read ten books, subscribed to magazines and journals, and started visiting galleries and artist studios. And I got the bug! Once I started to understand what went into art, it became clear to me that art was like music and artists were like songwriters. The more I stared at artworks, the more I could untangle their lines with my eyes and "feel" the work in my heart. The more I consumed art, the more I understood the intent of the artist. And as my curiosity exploded, the more passionate I became about the need to frame my business idea.

But then that little voice in my head kicked in. The one that says *you aren't going to succeed, this is a bad idea*, or *you are going down the wrong track*. You know it as self-doubt, and it is a real bitch. How can I do this with so many bills, personal challenges, and a lack of knowledge of the space? No matter how motivated I was to do something purpose based, I was still confronting the staggering reality that a real salary and a secure job might be the safest way to stabilize my life so I could focus on all my personal challenges. These were real concerns, but I knew I had to find a way to silence the negative talk and forge ahead toward my new goals.

I called up my friend Scott McGraw and invited him to lunch. Scott is one of the most thoughtful people I have ever met, a successful businessman, an early investor in School of Rock, and the soft-spoken, measured voice that I needed to lean on. Scott also came from the media business, and he was offering to set me up with some contacts to pursue jobs. I drove out to Summit, New Jersey, for lunch, and Scott and I got caught up in a discussion on life, family, and my job pursuits. He agreed to make some meetings happen for me where I could interview for executive roles. Before we left, like a real swami, Scott asked one more question: "Hey, what else have you been working on?"

I'm not sure how he found the intuition to ask that, but he must have tapped into some signals of restlessness and deep searching I was doing. I said, "I have been considering opening an art school." After that rolled off my lips, I paused and thought to myself, "I can't believe I just blurted that out. He must think I am crazy!" Just the opposite occurred.

As always, Scott asked a simple, calm follow-up question: "Wow, that's cool . . . Tell me more." I then went on a twenty-minute download, and as I spoke, Scott asked more questions. I could tell that the two of us were both getting excited about this concept that had no structure and, in a lot of ways, no basis to proceed. But, at the same time, it seemed to make sense to us. We both raised creative kids in suburbia who fell through the cracks because of the lack of compelling creative education in America.

Scott's daughter was studying art and photography at Skidmore College, and Scott was on the board of trustees there. He saw how great colleges like Skidmore were providing inspiring education, but he also reflected that he had always struggled with the challenge of finding a cool, credible place for his daughter to take recreational photography classes near her home in Short Hills, New Jersey. The two of them had to trek into Manhattan every Saturday so Carolyn could take classes, and he said to me that there was a real void in the marketplace.

After coffee and switching gears, we got the tab and Scott said, "I'm going to set you up for those calls, but keep me posted on that art school idea. If you want to do something, I'm in." I drove home that day knowing exactly what that meant. Scott wasn't gratuitous about how he phrased things. He would support me and invest some dough if I wanted to try to build an art school. When I got home, I called him and confirmed his intent.

One supporter. One believer. One bandmate. That is all I needed. These are the types of moments that are hard to manufacture. I'm going to share more about One River School later, but that early support paved the way. Today, we have fifteen schools in six states, and we are building a company with the goal of *transforming art education®* in America.

The main reason I'm providing the backstory of my life and what led to my launching One River is to clarify some essential points that will roll up as the primary drivers of this book going forward. As I carefully reviewed and studied how I got to the point of launching One River, I realized I could distill this into **five basic rules that govern our future.** These are for everyone with a dream or a goal or those embarking on a new endeavor. Universal in nature, they can be applied to your personal or professional life to pursue anything of meaning and value.

Here are the five basic premises that can govern our futures and drive growth:

1. **Take personal responsibility.**
   We are responsible for our decisions and our outcomes. Do not blame anyone; take full ownership.
2. **Know thyself.**
   If we don't take the time to diagnose what matters most to us and study what's working and what's not working, we will likely never find our true purpose and our most joyful state of mind.
3. **You can change.**
   We can reinvent ourselves at any time in our lives, and if we are committed, it is easier to do so as we age.
4. **Change is hard; not changing is worse.**
   Profound change will challenge you to the core. Complacency is often a slow road to misery.

5. **Be the creative person you are meant to be.**
   We all possess creative competence. We simply must learn to channel it to develop the right strategies to achieve our goals.

The process of better understanding myself in the middle of my life required me to analyze the specific things that I loved to do and the natural skills that were encoded in me from childhood. Reconnecting with your path is super important for framing your future, and I recommend it to everyone who is at a crossroads in their adult life. We all face complex struggles that can consume every aspect of our lives. I share the trajectory of my professional life against a backdrop of personal challenges so you can see the work I had to do on myself, which will create context for your life journey and the work you need to do.

In the next few chapters, I share the backstory and some intimate details about my life journey so that you can have a perspective of the personal and professional roads that I have traveled. And while my story might resonate with yours at some level, this book is not about me, but rather, written for you.

Later on, when we do some deep thinking about your future in part two, I hope that you also take the time to reflect on your past, including the hardwired traits you were blessed with, the things that brought you the most joy and defined you when you were young, the struggles that you faced, and the learnings that you accumulated along the way. These reflections are essential to rethinking what to prioritize in the future.

Now, we are about to experience the remarkable opportunity of understanding the forces that guide our behavior. We all have walked different pathways, and your own journey is as unique and special as any.

It is time to **Grow**, and from this point forward, **Folding** is not an option.

CHAPTER TWO

MY ROOTS

A Creative Soul at Heart

Every kid in the world responds to music. They hear the rhythm of their mother's heartbeat in the womb, and they start to groove with it. This primitive sound is then imprinted in our brain and our soul moments after conception. Growing up, I was fanatical about music. We had boxes filled with albums in our house—33s and our parents' old-school 78s. Playtime meant sifting through records and creating my own stack—the playlist of yesteryear!

My dad, Herb Ross, was so interesting: a garment center guy who was born in 1931 and raised by poor, immigrant, Polish-Jewish parents during the Depression era in the Bronx, New York. He was a cool street guy who was easy to get along with and could win people over with his genuine likeability. My dad was a jock, but he was also into music and grew up with the amazing Big Band era of the '40s that brought us Benny Goodman and others whose music was sweeping the country at that time. Jazz had morphed into something different, becoming the pop music of his day.

When I was growing up in the '60s and '70s, Dad was a complex character who demonstrated deep affection for his kids and his music. He became a lover of Motown and contemporary jazz, while always exploring other cool genres of music. We would drive in the car, and he would throw on Curtis Mayfield, George Benson, Herbie Mann, Al Green, Issac Hayes, or Bob Dylan—he had great taste, and it was always fun to listen to the radio and evaluate the new music of the day with him. He also displayed a hip fashion sensibility and a fun-loving exterior, but these traits were often masked by a deeply insecure and anxious interior.

On the other hand, my mom, Elaine Ross, was into the same music as most women of her age. Barbara Streisand and Johnny Mathis were at the top of her list, but she also crossed over and appreciated the great vocals of the Temptations and Four Tops. Black music was blowing up and our household was down with it. We were buying records from Stevie Wonder, Marvin Gaye, Barry White, and all the other cool crossover acts that were breaking out in America. Show tunes were also important, and my mom owned the soundtrack of the best Broadway musicals and the movies of our day. We had hours of fun playing tracks and singing along.

From the time I was a little kid, I played my parents' music for days on end. When I was about seven years old, I would take my weekly allowance and go to the store with Mom to buy records. My personal music journey was officially on the move, and rock and roll was entering its heyday. From 1968 to '78, which comprised my youth and teenage years from ages seven to seventeen, music went through a remarkable transformation with the rise of bands and what is now known as classic rock. I was in hook, line, and sinker!

Make no mistake, the Beatles were and always will be number one. I watched their movies, listened to their records, and was astounded by the international adulation for them. Right around this time, they were also going through their dysfunction, and you could see their pop idol cleanliness shifting to a hippie look, which was aligned with what I was seeing everywhere. It was 1968, and there was madness everywhere—

Vietnam, race riots, intense times, and a horrible economy. New York was filthy, dirty, unsafe, and a tough place to live. The world and our country were in chaos. Music seemed to put the edge of this era on its shoulders, and when the decade closed, we had Woodstock and the breakup of the Beatles as massive music news, while the headlines brought us staggering tragedies that included Kent State and the murders of MLK and RFK. It makes the discord of today seem mild.

All of this paved the way for the rock music of the '70s, and holy shit was I down with the program. The Stones were special, but to me the Who were the best. I heard *Tommy*, *Quadrophenia*, and *Who's Next*, and I was mesmerized. Then there was Clapton and Credence, The Doors, and the Allman Brothers. Not to mention Led Zeppelin, Deep Purple, Jimi Hendrix, and so many more artists who were generating memorable sounds. Rock and roll was busting out everywhere; it was tied to our pop culture and celebrated daily on the new FM radio. The inspirational music of these artists was changing the culture in America and worldwide.

But there was also some new stuff happening at Motown, and The Jackson 5 rocked my world. When I saw them perform "I'll Be There" on *American Bandstand*, I could not believe what I was watching. And of course there was Stevie Wonder! I saw Stevie Wonder at Madison Square Garden, my first concert, in 1974. He was rocking his tour to support the album *Fulfillingness' First Finale*, and thirteen-year-old Matty Ross was in the house. This album was the third record in a string of records that made Stevie, in my opinion, the number-one artist in the world at that moment.

You get the drift? While this book isn't about my musical escapades, I want to highlight how possessed I was with music. It was and remains an essential passion for me. Like all adolescent kids, as I was trying to find myself, the music of my era spoke to my heart and soul in a profound way. I also was wired with creative talent but was never really provided with any mentoring in this space. I stumbled on certain things and expressed my basic interests, taking advantage of resources that helped me activate some of the creative passion I felt.

Acting was also one of my earliest creative outlets. It began when I was a little kid, and I was often cast as the lead in our plays. Singing and acting were some of the most fun things about my childhood; I was fearless and loved to be part of delivering an experience for an audience. When my parents entertained on Saturday night, I came out and did impressions, sang songs, and enjoyed the attention of their friends. But, as I got older, something happened that has retrospectively stuck out in my head as the thing that shifted me away from performing forever.

I starred in a play in the sixth grade, and my parents didn't come to the show. It was weird for me because I worked so hard to be the Mad Hatter in *Alice in Wonderland*. All my friends' parents were there to support them. I don't tell this story because I want to share how sad I was. Oddly, I remember feeling more confused than anything else. I asked myself, *How come no one came?* That question led me to form this answer: *I guess acting's not that important*. In particular, my mom, and especially my dad, seemed disconnected from the value of acting, and, for that matter, the role creative education could play as a supporting tool for my growth and confidence. I never acted in another play for the rest of my life. This is something I deeply regret because I am certain I would have loved doing it, and it would have helped me grow. But, at the same time, I have used my creative talent in other ways, while developing strong relationships with friends and business associates and have always remained a playful guy who is comfortable wearing his emotions on his sleeve.

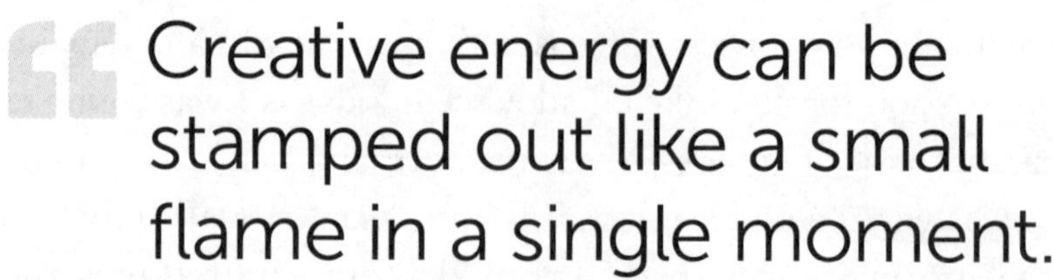

I don't think my parents meant to stifle my flame, but I couldn't see the value in acting without their support. All it takes is someone ridiculing you or questioning your talent. Humans are fragile and built to please. We also gravitate to what we are naturally good at and the things that bring us joy. It takes dogmatic confidence to open yourself up to share your creative side, and it takes parental and community support to help fast-track these skills. I have seen it across thousands of kids from my time as CEO of School of Rock to my current venture at One River School of Art and Design, a business built to *transform art education*®. In both settings, the difference that parents and friends make means everything.

Having said that, when you are young and you don't get the support, it is easy to vacillate and move on to the next thing. That is what I did. At twelve years old, I was wired for all the creative input I could get, but my parents in many ways were asleep at the wheel and stuck in their parental model of the post-Depression era. Sports dominated our household, and my dad would come home from work and talk/play sports with my brothers. So I did what a lot of young boys do, and I followed their interest in sports as well. I played hoops, tennis, and baseball and built great friendships on the streets of Queens as a result. I was pretty good and made the high school baseball team. I was one of the top bowlers in New York as well. But, at my core, somewhere deep inside me, there was an interest in the arts that was going to be suppressed for many years to come.

I took one more swing at creative expression when I was thirteen. I told my mom I wanted to play guitar. I was obsessed with music and this felt like a natural outlet for me. I could memorize lyrics and understood melodies, and the guitar that I was hearing all the time was flipping me out. I had to do this! Jimi Hendrix, Duane Allman, Frank Zappa, Eric Clapton, Jimmy Page, and Jeff Beck were becoming musical idols to me, and I dreamed of being on stage and playing like them. I begged my mom for a guitar, and she took me to Sam Ash to shop. I so badly wanted an electric guitar and amp, but Mom wasn't going for it since we lived in an apartment in Queens, and I shared a small room with two brothers.

"There's no room for that," she said, and I wound up buying an acoustic guitar and she agreed to get me some lessons.

We found a local teacher, and this dude came to my house once a week to teach me to play. For several reasons, I didn't love the experience. I would strum this guitar and work on technique while learning to play some of the sappiest songs—music that I couldn't respond to. Then he would leave, and I would throw my guitar under my bed and drop the needle on Led Zeppelin. That is what I wanted to learn to play! And, to make matters worse, Mom was always yelling at me to practice. It sounded like "do your homework" to my thirteen-year-old ears. I couldn't bear it anymore. I wanted this to be fun and personal to me, but I shut down and quit because it felt like another chore. "Wow, if I only had the School of Rock when I was a kid" was the phrase I heard constantly from parents when I was building that business, and it was something that I lived firsthand.

Let's review. I was singing and performing nonstop at home. In camp and in school, I was acting in plays and often getting cast in the lead role. I was even writing comedy sketches and doing impressions around the house. I was begging to learn music and passionate about learning to play the guitar. But, no matter how I expressed my interests, I couldn't find the proper mentoring, guidance, and resources. My parents were disconnected from the strategy of mining my individual strengths and needs. Today, it is quite common for each kid in a house to have an individualized development plan that focuses on their unique strengths. This was not common back in the day and not indicative of my folks' approach to raising us. We weren't wealthy. We were a middle-class family, and my parents were not educated and refined. They didn't go to college, and their upbringing never prepared them to provide the type of tools I was seeking.

To make matters worse, my folks had a horrible relationship, and my dad left home when I was fourteen. My high school years were a paradox for me. I loved my dad, but he left for another woman and broke my mom's heart. It was such a hard time for me because every day I came home from school, I found my mom in bed, crying and sick. On top of that, I was deeply insecure and searching to find myself. School always came easy to me, and I was distracted and bored. I was invited into a special program for gifted students and elected to skip eighth grade with a small cohort of kids. Since I was bored at school, I thought this was the right idea, and, weird as it may seem, I made the decision without any parental involvement. But, by the time I got to tenth grade, I realized that I was an immature, skinny kid with a facade of confidence, whose home was falling apart. My friends in high school became my family, and I threw my heart and soul into those relationships. They helped me mask the challenges I had in my head and the pain I was experiencing at home.

We had such a tight group in high school, and I was so lucky. "The fellas" helped me keep it real, and without my friends to lean on and connect with, I would have slid into depression. I was both anxious and happy at the same time. Cocky and angry. Confident and confused. Adolescence was a mixed cocktail of testosterone and the crazy street culture of Queens, New York, in the '70s, combined with maximum family dysfunction. All of this challenged me to develop massive perseverance to grind my way out. In high school, I struggled in silence and mastered the happy exterior face that the world around me came to know.

Ever felt that way? You find yourself in disarray even though the world, from the outside looking in, thought you were cool and doing well. But from the inside looking out, you were anything but that. Just steps away from possibly crashing, you fight through the pain while your adolescent brain is at battle with real-world, adult challenges. Guess what? You are not alone. We all face obstacles like this. Think of the times all you wanted was input, support, and mentorship but couldn't find it. So, you put your head down and relied on your instincts to sequence yourself from challenge to challenge, figuring it out along the way. Sure, you got through it. But not without a fair share of unnecessary struggle.

At fourteen, I had no one to lean on and somehow felt I was on my own. Don't get me wrong, my family loved me, and I felt that every day of my life. In fact, the go-to parental toolkit was 95 percent Jewish love and 5 percent screaming at me. My brothers and I were close, but they were much older, and I was often by myself. I was blessed to feel love and learned how to give love, but no one knew how to mentor and guide me. It was clear I was going to have to figure it all out on my own. When I was asked for my high school yearbook, "What do you want to be when you grow up?" only one word came to mind: *successful*. I had no idea which way to turn and what to do, but my mom always said to me, "Be a dentist." While I had no interest in science, her simple act of setting the bar high told me she fully believed in me. When I think back, it is weird how her little positive reinforcement helped provide confidence and motivation for me. As a result, I knew I had to pursue college, and I was going to be the first kid in my family to get a bachelor's degree.

I got the applications, filled them out, and inquired about and received loans and financial aid. I only applied to one school, Brockport State College. It was a no-brainer, as two of my best buds, Morris and Rob, went there a year ahead of me. "Moe" was raving about it when he came home for the first break in October: "Dude, they have a new $20 million gym, eighty bars, and parties every night." I was sold! Truth is, my best friend Claudio and I were also going to room together, and I knew I was going to be safe because I had four homies from Queens with me. They were my boys, and I was still not ready to let go. However, after six months at Brockport, I knew it was the wrong place for me. Everyone was there for the party, and it felt just like an extension of high school, with more freedom, eight hours from home. I decided to transfer to SUNY Albany, which was a game changer for me.

When you grow up, you have an insulated perspective of the world, often reflected by the community and people with which you grew up. In Queens, no one spoke about being a doctor or a lawyer, or anything for that matter. This was the way it was in Brockport. However, when I got to Albany, the pivot began because my peer group was totally different. These were largely kids who grew up in affluent suburbs like Long Island

and Westchester. They came from stable and educated households, and it was clear that they were all there to carve out a career path for themselves. Almost everyone was ambitious.

I escaped the confinement of the streets of Queens, and for the first time in my life, I was around people whose goals were high, who believed in themselves, and who were working to launch their lives with a committed mindset. I got into the car, put my foot on the gas, and was ready to roll. That is the remarkable thing about fostering growth—I was like a musician looking for a band, and I finally found a group of talented people who could help me reach the next level. I remember asking a couple of people what they wanted to do with their life, and I was confused when they told me they were going to medical school. My first reaction was, "You can't be a doctor because you are just like me." Then I realized something profound. They could do it simply because they believed in themselves! They wanted that outcome, and they were going to bust their asses to get there. This was a turning point for me, and it also became a profound lesson in the importance of peer modeling.

> "Surrounding yourself with the right people may be the most important driver of your success.

The rest of my college years were quite successful. I got into the business school at SUNY Albany, graduated *cum laude* with a degree in marketing, and went to work. I was driven to find a career path, pushed by the quality of the people around me, and all I had to lean on were my natural skills and drive to be successful. Somehow, I was going to figure out my options and deploy a professional strategy to help move beyond the classroom into the real world of business in New York.

Life, much like rock and roll, can be a disjointed setlist—filled with hits, deep cuts, and a few songs that don't quite land. But if there's one thing I've learned, it's that passion, persistence, and the right crowd can turn a simple tune into an anthem. Every riff, every creative spark that flickered, and every moment I felt unseen or unheard—those were just the opening chords of a much bigger song. But the truth is, talent isn't enough. You need support, belief, and a stage where your sound can be amplified.

I didn't have all of that in my early years, but I learned to hustle, remix my failures into lessons, and play louder until the world had no choice but to listen. A music career can mirror life itself. You start by jamming in a garage, you put in the hours, and suddenly, the music starts to flow. You get better. You get noticed. And if you keep at it, the crowd starts singing your lyrics back to you. But here's the real backstage pass: Who you surround yourself with will determine how far your song travels. The right people elevate your sound, push you to jam harder, and remind you why you picked up the instrument in the first place. When searching for an ambitious mindset to begin my career, I found my band at SUNY Albany, a group of driven people who played a compelling tune—and that changed everything.

So, if you're at that crossroads, if you're standing in the wings wondering if you should step into the spotlight, here's your cue: Play. Loud. Even if no one's listening at first. Keep going. Find your sound. Find your band. And when the world tries to drown you out, crank the volume and give them a show they'll never forget.

The encore is yours to write. Let's begin.

CHAPTER THREE

BUILDING PROFESSIONAL COMPETENCE

Radio 101

I sought out the dean of the business school during my final year at SUNY Albany to ask him for career guidance. I remember telling him that I had no idea what I wanted to do, and with no preparation or forethought, I blurted out, "I want to run a company one day." Thoughtfully, he said, "Most CEOs start in sales, so go get a job in sales." While I am not sure if his analysis was statistically true or if it holds up today, that simple nod pushed me out the door with a plan.

My father was an incredible salesman, and there was no doubt that I shared a lot of these traits. When I thought more about what made him special, I realized that he could connect and build trust quickly with almost anyone. Herb Ross' natural gift was his ability to make others feel better about themselves, and this allowed my dad to create great customer relationships, which gave him the license to recommend products and close deals. I shared this quality and felt certain I could follow in his footsteps. So, upon graduation, I went after it. But even armed with these traits, I was in store for a rude awakening.

When I graduated in December 1982, there were no on-campus interviews. So, like so many others, I simply had to jump in and figure it out. Back in those days, the *New York Times* Sunday classifieds was usually seventy-five pages thick and filled with job listings. But things were different in 1982, as we were in the middle of a massive global recession. Unemployment reached 11 percent and the United States experienced double-digit inflation. No one was hiring. Having said that, I was motivated to get in the game, driven by my need to get out of the house. So I took the first job I was offered, selling printing services. After six months of cold-calling and hating the process, I got into a retail management program for a men's custom clothing chain called The Custom Shop. The firm developed a fantastic management training experience that I thought would teach me how to connect with customers. And one of the coolest aspects of this opportunity was that our customers were almost always super high-achieving professionals, so I had a wonderful consumer base from which I could learn. I thrived at it.

I was twenty-two years old and developing personal connections with leaders in business and government. I was off and running, hardly worried that my peers were working in more prestigious jobs at more prestigious firms. This was my time to refine my skills and grow and polish my unsophisticated persona; for a kid from a broken home in Queens, this was my chance to work hard and learn, and I needed foundational skills to refine myself. I made shirts for and developed relationships with many amazing people, including Carl Icahn (one of the most successful M&A executives in the world), Rudy Perpich (the governor of Minnesota), the President of CBS, and countless others. Each unique engagement allowed me to build confidence and trust, and as I grew more confident, I tapped into my relationship-building skills to make my first real exciting professional pivot.

One day I met Gene Lothery, the head of CBS Radio's AM radio division, and I asked him to tell me more about what it was like to work in radio. He was the coolest guy ever, a super successful man who was clearly a pioneer as an African American in a senior executive role in the media business in the early 1980s. Gene was so smart and so good on his feet. He had this natural skill to make everyone around him feel like a million bucks. After I measured Gene for a shirt (and upsold him another six shirts with some ties to match), he said to me, "If you are ever interested in learning more about CBS Radio, give me a call and I will set you up with some meetings with various sales managers throughout our different radio platforms." While thinking about his comment a few days later, I picked up the phone and dialed his direct number at the office. Sure enough, he answered, "Lothery."

I said, "Hi, Gene, its Matt Ross from The Custom Shop. I have a question for you. When you were in, you said that you would set me up for some meetings. Were you serious?"

My naiveté and a little anxiousness showed through, but Gene was genuinely interested in me and said, "Of course I will do it!"

This was a special time in my life, but we cannot overlook the takeaways from these experiences. First, Gene was always looking for new talent for his business. Whether he was ordering food at a high-end restaurant or getting fitted for some shirts, he let inspiration guide him. Gene knew talent when he saw it and never let an opportunity to find his next team member pass. As a result of this early and important experience, I have made it my business to always recruit. Gene taught me that your next best employee may fall into your lap at any given time, so you better treat people well and always be on the lookout for exceptional talent.

Another crucial takeaway was that my ability to relate to all these super successful people was fueled by two things: *being myself* and *focusing on their needs*. People can always spot when someone is acting or trying too hard. I live by the mantra that you must make it about others instead of yourself. I learned this lesson at an early age, and I am thankful for it. There are just some lessons that stay with you no matter the circumstances. They transcend time and space, and they are like the chorus to an amazing track. Think about those similar lessons in your life—how have they guided you along the way?

Back to my job search, I bet you are waiting for me to tell you I got the job at CBS the next week and was off to the races as a media executive. Nope! It took me almost three years and over fifteen interviews with ten different people before I went to work at WCBS-AM in 1987! That's the way it goes sometimes—you must chip away at your goals until you get there. Nothing worth anything in life comes easy. When I reflected on all the exploratory interviews I went on at CBS, I realized that the people I met and the culture throughout the company were things with which I identified. It made me want it even more. Since I had a marketing degree and had now developed the corresponding persuasive skills, sales seemed like the right vehicle for me. I was right. By the time I got hired at CBS, I spent two-and-a-half years working for a trade publication in the apparel industry and I refined everything about myself. I studied what great salespeople did, took continuing education courses, read books, and applied myself with great results. I had lots of minor league experience, and I was ready to perform when I finally arrived at CBS.

It didn't take me long to start generating results. I was hungry to make money and was looking for recognition. While I was blessed with natural skills, I also developed a disciplined work ethic that was surprising even to me. I had always cut corners because school came easy for me. But I was motivated to grow and finally found my people. After two-and-a-half years of tremendous learning, I took a job working for Viacom as the national sales manager for their flagship radio station 106.7 Lite-FM, New York, and was responsible for managing all our clients based outside New York.

This felt like the major leagues, and I thought I made it. Traveling the country and entertaining national advertisers allowed me to broaden my sophistication. I overachieved every sales goal, and my direct boss loved me. But my general manager was a ruthless tyrant who lived to break people down and make them feel less important. It impacted my desire to remain at Viacom. From that experience, I learned there are really two types of leaders in this world: those that will make you want to run through walls and everyone else. Our GM was a former marine who was full of himself and had a disturbed persona causing him to lead by intimidation. He made it his business to show me that he was "the man" and unfortunately, I couldn't suck up.

It was becoming clear to me that great companies sometimes appeared great because of the power of their brands and their products. But, I had yet to work for a company with the type of culture that inspired me to dig in for the long term. I loved the radio business, which was growing at an exponential rate in the late '80s. But I wanted to find a company that would inspire me by how they treated their customers AND their employees. It seemed so clear to me that the way to build a great business was to inspire your people to work hard and have fun. To teach them and give them the tools to grow. To do what you say you would do as a leader. To allow employees to be themselves. To reward the hardest-working and best performers. To create standards of excellence so that the best and the brightest would be attracted to work for you. But it wasn't so simple to find this place. Let me set the stage for where I was on a holistic level.

If you are a in a leadership role, I cannot stress this path enough. You are only as good as the people you inspire to do their best work every day. Those that you can move to action. That is the trick. Anyone can hire anyone else. But moving people in a way that makes them give it their all every single day is something else. That is what I was looking for—inspiration, mentorship, a new home.

In 1991, at thirty years old, I also achieved one of my top goals when I completed an MBA in finance at NYU. I went part time at night for almost five years. The work I did to improve my understanding of business management enhanced my confidence. But as I was fine-tuning my skill set, I was also feeling unsettled in my job and viewed myself as a free agent looking to grow personally and professionally. I was just entering into a new decade of life and now had a body of work that helped me understand what I was good at and what I loved to do. I felt like I needed to identify a large professional challenge that would also require me to step out of my comfort zone. I wanted to find a mentor to help me refine my skills and allow me to grow dynamically, so I did what every born-and-bred, Jewish New Yorker did. I took a job as Director of Sales for three urban radio stations in the South and moved to Charlotte, North Carolina.

This was not a sitcom concept, but in many ways it could have been. I went to work for a start-up company called Broadcasting Partners Inc. (BPI) that seemed to be wired differently. They set the table for the challenges I would face and got out of the way. The late Wayne Brown, a former boss from CBS, hired me and quickly became a mentor and one of my dearest friends in the world. Wayne had the best people skills, and he was so real and inspiring. Wayne was an African American in the media business who was on the fast track and winning people over with a lovable personality, genuine kindness, and an interest in building employee-centric cultures. He needed a hardworking, focused sales leader who could help to break down the race barriers that prevented our radio stations from growing and getting our fair share of the advertising pie. My job was to build and lead a team to convince advertisers to spend their money targeting black consumers—it was a unique opportunity.

We were a dynamic team, and our parent company invested in a unique platform of tools that helped us hire talent with great precision and teach them to become world-class marketers and salespeople. The guys who ran the company, Lee Simonson and Barry Mayo, were veteran broadcasters who gave you the ball and allowed you to run with it. Unlike the big media companies for which I previously worked, BPI's leadership team was there to serve their employees as opposed to building a culture where the employees were there to serve their bosses. I was part of a customer-driven business that was rooted in an employee-centric culture, and this was an important turning point for me.

We should all feel as if we are a part of such a special organization. I felt as if I found my home, and it was an absolute pleasure to go to work. Gone were the days of suffering through unappreciative bosses, poisonous cultures, and lack of mentorship. Once I teamed up with Wayne and his colleagues, I knew I found an environment that could cultivate my talents. As a result, we hit home runs, and I helped to build some of the fastest-growing and most successful media properties in the country. I hired and mentored a team of talent that gave me the greatest professional gratification I had to date, and I became a real leader with real confidence.

Things were smooth, and I was starting to blossom as a media executive in this small and growing community. I was helping to bridge a social gap as a white man representing media properties that targeted black consumers, and I was personally advocating for and breaking cultural race barriers that were profound and deeply rooted. Even though Charlotte was growing, this was still the Old South, and I was a clear outsider. No one cared that I was Jewish, but I was a "Yankee" who had to work hard to erase barriers and build trust.

Part of BPI's toolkit was tapping into the business philosophy of some of the most dynamic leaders around. This led me to teachers like Stephen Covey and Peter Drucker. I still deploy most of the skills I learned from them in the early '90s and have even adapted some of these concepts into the growth toolkit that I will share more about later in this book. One of the main tenets that has served me as well as any other learning in life is a simple one:

> The best way to be understood is to be understanding.

Stephen Covey's philosophy[1] is simple on the surface, but it is rarely practiced. In essence, the first goal is to master how others think and what motivates them. If you want to build trust, break down barriers, motivate people, sell things, and lead others to generate massive results, this is where it begins. Said differently, "It's not about you; it's about them." I mastered the art of speaking softly and making connections that were not about me when I was on the ground trying to build trust in the South. I asked questions and listened well. I wanted to know where people came from, how they thought about life, what their goals were, what their perceptions were, and so on. I made sure that the "fast-talking New Yorker" would become a myth. The goal was to be likable and build deep relationships with everyone I met. Doing so allowed me to create profoundly important relationships based on real trust.

As I built the business and positioned myself for significant growth in the company, I was hit with a massive curveball that became a trend at the time in the radio industry. Our company was sold! I was finally working for people who understood me. I was making money, learning, and building significant leadership skills, and I wanted nothing more than to dig in and finally throw down some long-term professional roots with BPI. But now I had new bosses, and I was not feeling their culture. They told me to hang in there because we were a public company, we were going to be expanding, and I would have massive opportunities for growth ahead, but I was in my current role for almost four years and really needed the next-level challenge right away.

Navigating my next step was tricky. I was recently married, and my wife, Susan, was pregnant. I was recruited to move to Atlanta and decided that this would be the next chapter in my professional development. The next few years in Atlanta were so professionally frustrating. I didn't find the corporate culture that I had been part of at BPI, and it became very clear to me that no matter how much money I made, I was deeply committed to principles that seemed to be super hard to find. However, at the same time, I became a father. Susan gave birth shortly after I accepted a position in Atlanta and a switch went off for me the moment that happened. Up until that point, life seemed simple and carefree when compared to the audacious challenge and responsibility of being a father. Everything was now more serious. I was deeply motivated to be the best father I could be, and I was fortunate to have an incredible partner in Susan.

We were best friends; we shared music and laughter; she was honest and caring; and she was someone who I learned a lot from. Susan also didn't suffer fools easily and she challenged me in a way in which I needed. All the stress and dysfunction of growing up in a broken family taught me many bad lessons, and I had to study what not to do. For instance, I had to learn to save money and the challenge of entertaining and the fast-track/demanding media business was hard to balance at times. I was anxious and worried, and this was just the start of challenges to come.

CHAPTER FOUR

CATASTROPHIC CHALLENGE

Life's Wake-up Call

We often face challenges that can derail our journeys, create obstacles along the way, and cause us extraordinary pain that might otherwise feel insurmountable. Perhaps you've been there before? Maybe you couldn't even think there would be light in all the darkness. These wake-up calls can come in many flavors, and sometimes they come in bunches. I've been there. I know how you feel. But faced with these challenges, we also get the chance to show just how strong we are. To allow our heart, our spirit, and our fight to drive us ahead and absolutely thrive.

That is, in many ways, where my catastrophic challenge begins.

The phone rang, and Susan looked over at the clock. It was too early for a phone call. Six o'clock in the morning to be exact. She answered the phone with a slight amount of trepidation, expecting bad news because, well, good news doesn't come before coffee. Her mother, Mary, was on the other end of the line, and I could tell there was a real issue. Susan's parents were visiting from New York, and we had spent the night at a hotel for a staycation, leaving our son Alex with my in-laws for the evening.

Susan quickly hung up the phone and said something was wrong. Mary was a very simple woman from Croatia and couldn't communicate the depth of what was happening, but she did explain Alex was nonresponsive and was having trouble breathing. We threw our stuff in our car, and I drove as fast as I could to get home, assuming he was fine but just a little groggy. Upon our arrival, it was anything but that. When we got there, Alex was completely catatonic and locked in a static state. We grabbed him and drove over one hundred miles per hour to the closest hospital. Doctors and nurses worked furiously on Alex. It seemed to be life or death—he wasn't getting enough oxygen, and the ER team looked terribly unsettled while frantically poking, prodding, and monitoring our baby boy.

I rubbed his leg and talked to him while Susan rubbed his forehead and whispered into his ear. They pumped him with valium and administered a battery of procedures. At this point, I estimated that he was in this state for over two hours. In hindsight, my mother-in-law should have called 911 immediately, but she never saw anything like this and didn't know what to instinctively do. After twenty-five minutes in the ER, and with Alex still locked in a nonresponsive state, the doctor turned to me and said they were going to intubate him and administer a tracheotomy. I was horrified and scared, but I started talking to Alex and rubbed his head, begging him to snap back to consciousness. Miraculously, he responded just moments before they began the procedure. My boy was coming out of the darkness, and the intensity of the room subsided. I cried like a baby. I knew we could have lost Alex that night.

Our son Alex was not like other kids. Born on January 9, 1995, Alex was our firstborn, our honeymoon baby, and the beginning of a blessed new life with my wife, Susan. But something seemed askew shortly after Alex's birth. We couldn't quite tell you exactly what was off—both Susan and I had not spent a lot of time around babies. Intuitively, though, we both knew that Alex was behaving differently than other children his age.

Every night I would race home after work, literally driving as fast as I could to see Alex before he went to bed. We were living in Atlanta at the time, moving there from Charlotte, North Carolina, sixty days after welcoming Alex into this world. I was so happy to be a father, and I treasured my half hour of quiet time with him before Susan put him down for the night. At the time, I remember Alex doing repetitive things. It started with him staring endlessly into a book and flipping the pages without displaying much emotion, trying to read them, or responding to the pictures. I would stand over him and talk to him, but he wouldn't look up. I remember giving him the nickname of "Alex the Ignorer." I was fascinated by how he would be so lost in the book that he could block out my voice entirely. One side of me thought his love for books was a blessing. The other side of me thought that something was wrong: What kid doesn't respond to sound?

We also watched Alex run in circles, rarely engage with other kids, struggle with sensory issues, and display other tendencies that were just different. Our pediatrician, who always said, "Don't worry, he's a boy and that's the way boys are," finally decided to give Alex a hearing test. Something wasn't adding up. We brought Alex in for an ABR test, a sophisticated method for checking brain waves related to sound. He passed. Alex could hear great. In fact, he could hear better than most. Hmm. Then how come a bomb could go off right next to him and Alex would remain locked in a fixed, nonemotional, repetitive stare? Something didn't add up.

After the hearing tests, doctors sent us to the Marcus Center in Atlanta because he was now about eighteen months old, and his language skills were virtually nonexistent. He continued to demonstrate other concerning behaviors as well: He was not social, displayed odd gestures, and struggled behaviorally. Even so, the doctors assured us he was "just a boy" and going to outgrow these things. While waiting to see a doctor and therapist at the Marcus Center, Susan and I looked up and saw a poster on the wall about autism. This was 1997, and there was very little information about autism in the general community. The poster said, "If your child has more than five of these twelve attributes, then they may have autism." Alex had almost all twelve! I turned to Susan, and she looked me in the eye. We started to cry. Alex had autism. *The full spectrum.*

In that moment, our world changed forever.

At the time, the literature said autism was a rare developmental disorder with an incidence rate of one in ten thousand. There was no cure. There were virtually no resources. We were living in Atlanta, and I wasn't happy at my job. We had no family there and few friends. Life crashed in on us. The prevailing thought at that time was if you bombarded your child with early intervention—behavioral, sensory, nutritional, and other interventions—you could help them escape this "solitary confinement of the brain." *We jumped in with a mission to save our kid and we threw our entire heart and soul into this battle.*

Over the next two years, Susan and I set up an early education program at home. This meant round-the-clock, one-on-one sessions for Alex and his therapists. We turned our basement into a special ed preschool, and we emptied a lot of our bank account to do everything we could to "save our child." All the literature we read said that there was proof we could "cure" Alex of autism if we provided massive early intervention. So day turned to night and weeks turned into months. I continued to grind at work, trying to provide for my family and ensure our boy had everything he needed. The pressure was staggering, and it started to have a real effect on my mental health. My persistent anxiety now turned to a more severe state of constant worry, and I started to develop some symptoms that flat-out scared the shit out of me. I had my first full-fledged panic attack. This was nothing like I ever felt before. My heart started racing, and I started to sweat and feel lightheaded. No matter what I tried to do, I couldn't escape the feeling of doom. It went away after about ten minutes. I remember telling Susan about what happened and how scared I was.

I saw a doctor who prescribed an SSRI medicine shortly after that. I was reluctant to take it and ended up choosing not to do so. I didn't want to take any drugs. I thought I could solve this on my own. After two months of attacks, including one that occurred in an airport on a business trip that had me almost in tears, I went back to the doctor. Very simply, my brain chemistry was out of balance. The catastrophic challenge of raising a boy who was now two-and-a-half years old and couldn't speak was beyond anything I imagined. On top of that, we had a second child, I was experiencing conflict at work, and my overall intensity level was through the roof. I was a powder keg without solutions, and the world was caving in on me.

As I reflect on all of this, it is almost surreal to revisit this period of my life. Without a doubt, I suffered from post-traumatic stress disorder and felt like I was slipping away as I watched my son show limited growth despite every possible intervention we provided. We were far from home with no family to support us, and I was scared to go to sleep and scared to wake up because I didn't know when the next panic attack would occur. I went back to the doctor and agreed to try Paxil. The clouds parted in just ten days of using it.

It was so strange . . . the medicine interrupted the loop I was in and allowed my system to reset. I also started some therapy. For the first time, I was committed to getting help for things that I couldn't fix on my own. Throughout life, I had dealt with my problems by simply putting my foot on the gas. If I worked harder, studied harder, and played harder, I would overcome my challenges by figuring out and executing a thoughtful solution. I would stay in motion so that my energy would be used as a force to combat the enemies in my head: worry, anxiety, fear, stress, and the fucking unknown that may get me!

While I was beginning to work on myself, I also went to work on my career by switching jobs, and my professional life was now on a strong track. Work became an outlet for me that allowed me to take all the negative energy that had built up inside me and apply it in a positive direction. I was now a general manager of a radio station for the first time, and, in my late thirties, I had become a rising leader in the radio industry. I led a complete turnaround of three radio stations in Atlanta, and my résumé demonstrated that I rebuilt two different broken businesses and created hundreds of millions of dollars of shareholder value for the companies I worked for. Along the way, as I refined my leadership skills, I also sharpened my strategic thinking and became quite confident in my ability to build businesses. That is when John Fullam called.

I knew John from BPI. He was overseeing a group of radio stations in New York, and he said the magic words to me: "How would you like to move back to New York to run the classic rock station Q104.3?" Holy shit! John offered me my dream job. Running a radio station in New York was the holy grail in my business, only twenty or so people had that job. My hometown! The music I loved! A growing company with a great boss! This seemed like a no-brainer. I was in. Then, John said, "By the way, it is also the worst-performing station in our company, and you have one year to fix it, or we are blowing it up." LOL. Okay, I should've added that part, but in a weird way, I completely identified with fixing broken businesses at that point. I accepted the challenge, and there could not have been a more important time in my life to get home.

It was a blessing to get Alex to New York to tap into the medical community, educational resources, and family support that could help us. And I needed to work for someone who believed in me and appreciated my entrepreneurial style. John was a soulful, spiritual, and amazingly calm guy who was the perfect boss. We both believed that you built great businesses through thoughtful talent selection and compelling leadership. We were committed to creating a fun, employee-centric culture that wasn't petty and provided real emotional engagement and financial rewards for the team. I knew that it was going to be hard to cut through the clutter and rebrand a business that was struggling, but I was certain that I was up for the task. John handed me the ball and let me run with it.

Guess what? *Within two-plus years, I led the largest turnaround of any radio station in the country during that period.* We quadrupled sales and went from a breakeven business to generating over $20 million in annual cash flow. It was fun, and I was getting recognition. I made *Crain's Business's* "40 Under 40" list of executives in New York. We were doing amazing things on air and in the community. Over the next few years, Clear Channel Radio promoted me to Senior Vice President of Sales in addition to my role as VP and GM of Q104.3. I was now overseeing a team of two hundred people that was generating almost $400 million in revenue, and I was positioned to continue to grow and succeed within the media business.

Then things changed in a minute.

9/11

I was in the middle of leading a sales training session in midtown Manhattan for twenty new account executives when someone walked in and said, "Matt, someone accidentally crashed into the World Trade Center." My immediate thought was *this wasn't an accident.* That's because I drove down the West Side Highway that morning, and I remember thinking at the time that it was the most beautiful and clear day I had ever seen. Visibility was never better—this was no accident. After the second plane crashed into the World Trade Center, and then in Pennsylvania and another into the Pentagon, I thought World War III had begun. My brain kicked into survival mode. I left our location on West Forty-Fourth Street and walked over to meet with my staff at Q104.3.

I surmised that if we were under attack, our nondescript building at Forty-Sixth Street and Sixth Avenue would not be a high-profile target and told everyone to stay in place. But, after a couple of hours passed, everyone was antsy to get home, so we all gave each other a hug and left the office, even though there was almost no way to get off Manhattan Island. I remember walking the street to my car and watching people crying uncontrollably, while others looked like zombies, in a mixed state of fear and disbelief. I was truly worried that I would never see my wife and kids again; I literally had no information about what was happening and how I was going to get home. There was no way to reach anyone, as all cell service was out. But I finally got to my car and began a ride that turned from the usual one-hour commute to one that lasted over eight hours. I was safe and lucky, but I was overwhelmed with what had happened only walking distance from me. The world changed on a dime, and in many ways, 2001 was also the beginning of a significant shift within the industry that I loved.

By 2002, we were at war in the Middle East, the economy was in free fall, the dot-com bubble burst, and it became clear to me that my industry was going to change. The radio business that I had seen thrive and prosper over the previous fifteen-plus years was now under attack as well. Broadband internet was creating alternative media tools, the iPod had changed how people bought and consumed records, the record industry was in shambles, consumer habits were changing, and terrestrial radio was going to have to reset itself. The business that I grew up in was never going to be the same.

Shortly thereafter, in 2002, we laid off thousands of people from Clear Channel Radio, and I declined a significant promotion that would have required me to move to Chicago. My son was in crisis, and I needed to continue to focus on creating stability for my family. So I transitioned to a senior executive position in New York with Emmis Radio, helping to run Hot 97 and two other stations. My leadership skills were now fine-tuned, and from 2002 to 2005, I succeeded in leading another substantial turnaround project in the media space. But, amidst all the change that was happening around me, I started to reflect more on my professional growth, from my twenties to my early forties.

I created a cool exercise and documented my *professional inventory*, those strengths and skills that I acquired over the years. Since I thought it was finally the right time for me to transition beyond the radio industry, I had to build a map of where I was and where I wanted to go. In doing so, I decided to analyze which skills I could transfer to other industries. I also thought about my passions and built an inventory that would inform the next stage of my professional life.

Here was my **professional inventory** in 2005:

- proven track record of building and leading teams
- lifelong learner—passionate about personal growth and development
- positive style; committed to lifting others up and creating a fun work culture
- skilled at mentoring and helping people uncover their best talents
- leader with a refined strategic skill set and a counterintuitive sensibility
- adept at uncovering opportunities and building plans to achieve outcomes
- creative thinker with a solid brand-building toolkit
- sales-oriented leader who thrives on high-performance orientation
- energized by big challenges and some thoughtful risk
- passionate and curious

Now that I was in my early forties, I felt I had to break out of a traditional corporate career. I simply wasn't political enough to make it to the top of a large, bureaucratic organization. After many years at large public companies, I saw many missed opportunities and countless moments where systems and processes got in the way of strategy and performance. While I made a great living and effectively navigated these, I wanted the next twenty years to allow me to control my personal destiny and find a more autonomous leadership role.

Up to this point in my life, I never had the financial resources to take such a risk. Because of that, I never spent much time thinking about starting a business. The personal and financial demands of raising a young family with a severely disabled child required predictable income. I also knew that I couldn't afford any more stress—entrepreneurship = uncertainty = maximum stress. So I started to spend hours dwelling on my strengths and my passions. I loved selling intangible products like advertising and building marketing concepts to help companies grow their brands.

> Why not build a music brand?

I started to test an artist management concept and signed an undiscovered musician named Carl Restivo. Carl became a kid brother whom I mentored and invested in. I was able to open some important doors that accelerated his career and growth. I got Carl signed to a recording contract with Wyclef Jean of the Fugees, who was building a label with Jay Records at the time. Carl immediately jumped into a Wyclef project and wound up writing, arranging, singing, and playing guitar on Wyclef's album *The Preacher's Son*. It was so much fun being part of that process and watching Carl grow and thrive. We signed a music publishing deal, Carl got paid a substantial amount for recording and writing with Wyclef, and I was excited about the potential course of my new career.

Then, out of the blue, Carl sent me a text: "How would you like to be the CEO of School of Rock?" I had no idea what he was talking about.

School of Rock was a great movie starring Jack Black that I saw about five times, but I was really confused and didn't understand what Carl meant. I knew he was teaching music for some guy and remembered thinking how crazy it was that I was getting job leads from my young artist. After further inquiry, Carl told me about the school's Founder, Paul Green, who was a unique guy based in Philly. Paul had five locations and lots of ambition, and I trusted Carl's intuition enough to take a meeting with Paul and started to research the music education space on my own.

> This was a strange time in my life.
> Change after change stacked up with more change.
> Have you ever been there before?

Finding yourself at a crossroads of struggle, of adversity, of challenge. Or perhaps a fateful decision between two amazing opportunities. You see, that is the beauty of change—it comes in many different flavors. Just like music, change has something for everyone.

Life can give us a wake-up call in many different forms and fashions. A sick child. A career disruption. Lost love. Any type of end or beginning. A midlife crisis. The list goes on and on and on. But as we face these challenges, the responsibility unequivocally lies with us to accept the challenge, accept the change, and find the optimal path through it.

So, let's continue.

CHAPTER FIVE

THE SCHOOL OF ROCK

and Rocked to the Core

It was fall 2005, and Joe Roberts, the Chairman of School of Rock, invited me to see a show that their New York students were putting on. Joe and I had some recent conversations where he confirmed the school was looking for a CEO, and I was intrigued by the idea. While I was a music fanatic my whole life, I was uncertain because I knew nothing about building a music education venture. The company had developed a simple and differentiated approach to music education for K–12 that focused on teaching them to play AND perform live. I reflected on my own painful guitar lessons and thought this was a novel idea.

So let me set the stage for you. I'm standing in a jam-packed venue in New York: the *iconic* CBGB. The excitement in the air was electric. This was a kid's concert? It felt way different! The students were about to play a tribute to Led Zeppelin. "Zep" was one of my favorite groups of all time and a band I had the blessing of seeing in their prime in 1977 at Madison Square Garden. I went that night expecting to see some kids trying their best and struggling with Jimmy Page's riffs and Robert Plant's vocals. Holy shit was I wrong. The simple "recital" was anything but a recital. It was a real rock and roll show on CBGB's stage, starring kids and teens! Some of them were outrageously good, and some were performing their way through their first show. I walked around and talked to parents, and the response was overwhelming. They told me that School of Rock *changed their kid's life*. This was a theme that parents around the country later shared with me constantly, and one I experienced in my own household for years to come.

I left that show a different person. It is hard to imagine that watching kids play a two-hour set of music would have such a profound effect on me, but *it changed my life*. Joe Roberts and I connected the next week, and we started having meaningful conversations about their vision, the needs of the business, my background, and my ability as a leader. I reflected on my **professional inventory** and the fact that I had spent twenty years building and fixing radio properties and refining skills in leadership, management, marketing, and sales. I was convinced that leaving radio and finding a new pathway where I could apply my skills to building an entrepreneurial venture seemed right for me, but one thing stood in the way: *the risk*.

> "The topic of risk is a profound one that tugs at all our insecurities and anxieties, and, at the opposite end of the spectrum, our motivations, wants, and desires.

No one wants to invite dramatic risk into their lives because it can be a scary proposition. But great reward is often the fruit of taking risks.

That is not to say we should behave recklessly in our risk assessment. That is hardly what I am saying. But a little bit of calculated risk can go a long way in building a pathway to achieving our dreams and reaching our goals. Living a life without risk is almost as detrimental to your growth as living one filled with it. Like anything, you need to find the right balance of taking chances and acting conservatively.

Here is the School of Rock business scenario at the time. The company had recently expanded to New York and San Francisco and operated five units in total, with two licensed partner schools in the fold. They had no franchise business and a few older licensed schools that had failed, and the operational and training tools were nonexistent. The Founder, Paul Green, demonstrated erratic behavior that offset his brilliance. He had built a dysfunctional and frenetic atmosphere that made it difficult to manage a business, and the company was struggling at a massive level.

No commitments were pending from any new investors, and, given the burn rate, School of Rock was projected to be out of cash in two-and-a-half months. The franchise business was still in predevelopment. There was no formal business plan; there was no corporate staff, no office, and there were tremendous challenges facing every school but one. Over lunch in New York, Paul walked me through the business model by drawing out the school unit economics on a napkin—yes, the old napkin sales pitch!—and Paul was a master at spinning a tail.

Even though this was going to be a gigantic challenge, something was telling me that this was the right time for me to lean on my entrepreneurial skill set. The hell with the risk! I jumped in with my whole body. I took out a line of credit on my home and made a substantial investment in the company. From my perspective, I was going big or not going at all. Since I was going to be responsible for building and executing the growth strategy, in effect, I was making a significant bet on myself and, in some ways, just as much a bet on School of Rock. At this stage of my professional life, *I was ready to meet the moment and throw my heart and soul into a career shift outside of the media business.* Besides all the potential financial benefits that could be derived long term, I was motivated to *grow* and challenge my intellectual capacity to build a nuanced and subtly complex business.

It's Time to Rock.

In October 2005, I joined School of Rock and finalized the formation of our franchise business. I became the CEO of the company and began the journey of trying to fix and build a business that provided a profound "creative educational experience." Prior to my arrival, there were a couple of bodies who were briefly appended to a CEO title, but there was never a CEO providing true leadership, driving strategy, developing operational excellence across the system, raising capital, developing talent, and doing everything else the company needed. This became my professional mission and passion.

It took a lot of emotional commitment to do this, and I ran hard in the face of risk and uncertainty at a time when my life was begging for certainty and stability. In addition to all the new professional challenges I was facing, Susan and I were fighting our greatest fight of all at home. Given that I had a son struggling with a lifelong and profound disability and a marginal nest egg to rely on, the rational and logical decision was to pass on School of Rock and join a company with a stable balance sheet. The simple logic said that I should follow my media friends into the digital media space and grab the best executive role I could find—one with a secure paycheck from a company that had significant financial backing—invest in my 401(k), pay down my mortgage, and start to turn toward my fifties with more stability.

But simple logic wouldn't help me grow in a meaningful way. Fuck that!

I was now entering middle age and was frustrated with the idea of simply "taking a job." I knew I had a gene for building things. Life was too short, and rock and roll was calling! I had seen hundreds of rock shows throughout the years, and music was an essential drug for me. My experience running Q104.3 in New York allowed me to align my professional challenge with my love for rock and roll once before, and now I was inspired because I saw things at School of Rock that flipped me out. The School of Rock taught kids to play Frank Zappa! In my mind, that shit was not possible. I was one of those strange cats that fell in love with this music as a teenager, and I saw Frank in concert thirty times. I thought that it was too hard, too weird, and not melodic enough for kids to get it. But they did! I was amazed by the creative outcomes School of Rock was generating across the board, and I thought I could guide the business to a new level of success.

When I arrived at School of Rock, I made sure to quickly identify the major business challenges, working as fast as I could to stabilize our business, raise capital, and refine our execution. For example, we had no corporate infrastructure, our technology toolkit was horrible, and we spent very little money on consumer marketing. However, I was able to find and close new franchise deals and emphasize growth, while investing in proper training and operating best practices. It was such a grind, and I worked seven days a week trying to establish our platform as the national leader in music education for kids. And my efforts paid off.

We were wildly successful in scaling our platform and built an impressive story that I couldn't be prouder of today, notwithstanding the early-stage challenges that we fought through. I raised millions of dollars in capital from 2005 to 2009, growing the platform from seven to fifty-five schools, securing incremental franchise deals that turned into another fifty schools, and leading the business to become the largest performance-based music school in the world for kids and teens. The economy was thriving during the first few years, and I was able to raise cash and grow our network substantially. I deployed all of the skills I developed over the first twenty years of my career and started to build a real company with widespread distribution across America and Mexico. I was passionate about building a unique consumer experience that was built on "sublime music education," and we took advantage of Paul's dogmatic promotional skills to tell the story to the media, while letting our kids demonstrate our magic on stage. It was inspiring, but we had challenges that were greatly accelerated when the winds of the Great Recession started to blow in 2008. Our access to capital started to dry up, and we had a lot of young schools that had not yet turned the corner to profitability.

Since capital was and always is key for a young company, I engineered the sale of our business to Sterling Partners in 2009. The world was in a tailspin, and this was clearly the best opportunity available to us to stabilize our balance sheet and allow us to continue to grow and professionalize our platform. I reset the business and built a new leadership team, but in 2010, after five years of giving my all to School of Rock, Sterling and I were not a perfect fit and agreed to part ways. Sterling built the Sylvan Learning centers chain, and they were tough people to work with who barely invested any time in understanding the nuances of our culture and the connection that I had developed with our employees and franchise partners. My exit as CEO from School of Rock was not exactly what I wanted, but I remained a significant investor in the company and continued to own franchise locations in New Jersey that were among the top-performing schools in the system.

This change was super hard for me, but I also fully understood that it was now their company, so we parted ways amicably, and I was left at a crossroads that so many people in middle age struggle with. Much like risk, change is a common part of life. It can happen to us, because of us, or, as we often find out, despite us. No matter how change comes into our lives, it is crucial to embrace it. Otherwise, it's like playing an out-of-tune instrument and producing disjointed sounds. You must learn to make a thoughtful pivot in the face of complex change and tap into your skills and tools to drive a confident shift.

I am eternally grateful for the School of Rock experience because it lit a torch in me that shines bright today. As I rolled into 2010, I once again faced some critical decisions to make about my life that felt like 2005. Do I take a job that would provide me with a salary and security while avoiding any new risk? Sound familiar? Again, I wasn't sure what to do. While everything in the world was off the rails as we recovered from the recession, and common sense was again yelling, "Take a job," I had so identified with the purpose of School of Rock that I begged for another chance to do something as meaningful. I looked at our kids, parents, and staff as one tribe, and I was in awe of the lives we changed through music education. Equally important, I had proven that I could live with substantial risk and excelled at building a new and unproven venture.

I spent more time reflecting on what the School of Rock professional experience did for me and why the purpose was life changing. School of Rock had something special. We taught rock and roll to kids! From the Who and the Stones to Motown, punk rock, funk, prog rock and everything in between. School of Rock taught kids to play and perform and put them on real stages in real rock venues to gain one-of-a-kind experiences that you can only feel on stage. It was magical. I saw it through the lens of a marketer who had run radio stations for many years, including the largest classic rock station in the country. I saw it as a person obsessed with music from birth. I saw it as a dude who wanted to play and perform as a kid and would have been a hardcore School of Rock student if it were available to me!

I also used another critical and personal lens to look at my School of Rock experience, which had a deep effect on me as well. My son Jason was seven years old when I joined School of Rock, not thriving at sports, and begging me to play guitar. He was struggling socially, and I could tell that he wasn't the alpha male or most confident kid on the block. However, there was something interesting about him that I had observed for years.

When Jason was a little boy, he had a speech delay, and we were concerned that he was also on the autism spectrum, but he wasn't. We put a bear hug around his developmental plan and got him early intervention. We had our functional PhD on the importance of early education through our challenges of raising Alex, and we were committed to providing the most appropriate resources to help Jason grow. He spoke gibberish at two years old, and we were scared. But he sang the Beatles—I kid you not! He could barely form sentences but was emotionally connected to music and moved by creative rhythm and lyrics. He was passionate about listening, playing with toy guitars, and mocking the videos we played on our DVDs.

I remember one day watching a DVD of the Who and looking over at my two-and-a-half-year-old son who was swinging his arms in toy-guitar windmills à la Pete Townsend. I never forgot the thought that had passed my mind in that moment: *There was something profound that music did to his brain, that tapped into an emotion and feeling that seemed to create something that felt special to him.* I also remembered watching a video back in the day of Tiger Woods at three years old, swinging the golf club on the *Mike Douglas Show* (Google this—it is the best). To be clear, I didn't think Jason would be the Tiger Woods of music. But, I was thinking how profound it was that Jason's brain was so naturally wired to connect with music in such a visceral way that it provided him with an undeniable chemical response of positive emotion and feeling. I really did think that at the time. So, when Jason turned eight years old, I brought him to see a show, and the look on his face was amazing. I asked him if he wanted to visit the New York school with me, and we signed him up for guitar lessons. Jason's addition to the School of Rock would also allow me to have a first-person, test-tube experience as a parent and consumer, and I was so excited to see how he would do in this new space, which was sort of like travel sports meets music education.

When I watched kids at our rock schools, I could tell that there was something tribal about our experience. This music club for kids attracted people who were often a little different, shy, and creatively inclined. It allowed them to connect with others through the common passion of music. It was fun. It was real. It was team centric with a chance to be an individual, too. It drove core values like hard work and practice and overtly rewarded them. The camaraderie and connections created at every School of Rock location were exceptional, and the growth, learning, and confidence we provided these kids through a shared educational experience were incredible.

So, in January 2006, Jason was in the game, and that June he played his first show—a tribute to AC/DC! At CBGB! Jason was a natural; he was fearless in a way that I hadn't seen in him before, singing and playing guitar on two songs. His little eight-year-old face was joyful as he stood on stage with a handful of kids from the School of Rock AllStars group. I could sense that he felt like he belonged. The switch went on, and I could see that my son was hooked. Our journey into the joy of learning to play music was activated.

Jason stayed at School of Rock for ten years. He took lessons and performed in each season in two different schools and show productions. By the time he left after high school, he had actually played *over three hundred live shows on stage*! He also achieved a massive goal by auditioning and being chosen to tour with the School of Rock AllStars four times. Jason played in venues around the country, including Lollapalooza, and had the insane experience of playing live with professional artists such as Perry Farrell from Jane's Addiction, Robbie Trujillo from Metallica, and Butch Trucks of the Allman Brothers, among others.

I am proud of him and his fight to overcome his own teenage social insecurities to become a wildly accomplished musician. Today, Jason is working on the dynamic challenge of becoming a touring musician, writing, recording, and playing live with his band Moon Sand Land among other projects, while also developing his business skills. I am in awe of his commitment to his craft and humble sensibility, which has never been motivated by the spotlight. Music saved my son's soul, and the personal mission piece for me was clear. While building School of Rock, I also helped Jason find himself. He became more confident daily while playing and creating sublime music and was empowered to overcome his insecurities. My personal life and professional purpose had merged, which was enlightening.

So, as I tried to figure out my next steps after School of Rock, I ran hard in the face of risk and uncertainty again, at a time when my life was begging for certainty and stability. As they say, the second you get comfortable, life throws you a curveball. I wish it were solely a professional curveball, as I could easily navigate that challenge. While I struggled with the economy and the challenge of identifying a new opportunity in the marketplace, Alex was working through his teenage years, and his profound autism was starting to turn into an experience that is almost impossible to share and to understand. At this very moment, when I was out of work and sorting out my career, Susan and I had our lives turned upside down in a much more significant way.

Alex had a complete psychiatric breakdown over three months that nearly destroyed him and us. Few people in the world can understand what it is like to raise a profoundly autistic son. Alex's inability to speak prevented him from telling us about the noise in his head and his frustration as a teenager. While Alex was nonverbal and tortured by it, he had the same feelings and emotions that we all have, but they were bottled up without a method to release them other than a massive breakdown. Puberty was something we weren't prepared for, and it wound up taking our boy away from us.

It is still incomprehensible to think about it and hard to describe to this day.

On top of his profound autism, Alex turned bipolar. He was unraveling and became violent with us and himself. One day, outside the doctor's office in New York, Alex stripped himself naked in a parking lot and went into a wild tantrum attacking me and Susan. Over the next week, in this altered and profoundly challenging state, my boy literally tore the hair out of his head in frustration and rage. We finally got Alex to an emergency room in New York, and our doctors at Columbia University went to work on finding an inpatient program to help stabilize him. After a few days, a bed opened at a facility in Westchester that dealt with teens in crisis. It was populated mainly with suicidal teens and others with deep psychiatric disorders, and Alex was the only person there with severe, nonverbal autism. *One side of me thought that we lost him forever.* But my optimistic side told me we had to rely on the medical experts who were terrific in their support.

Susan and I did our best to withstand the stress and uncertainty, and with the intervention of the right medicines for Alex, the storm clouds passed, and our loving and beautiful son returned to the special boy that we knew. Alex wound up coming home two weeks later, and six months after that, he entered a residential school in Maryland, where he stayed until age twenty-two. Today, Alex is in a group home in New Jersey, and *we are grateful every minute of every day that he demonstrated the perseverance to fight through his compelling challenges.* There have been countless people who have helped him be the best he could be, and without them, it's possible that we would've had a catastrophic outcome. Susan and I are forever grateful for the community that has supported Alex and our family during our lifetime and believe these folks will have the E-Z Pass to heaven.

There are moments in your life that rock you to your core. Moments that force you to stop, take a deep breath, and reevaluate what truly matters. In these moments of crisis, we realize how much strength we hold, often more than we ever believed possible. But these moments are also reminders that we don't have to walk through storms alone. Just as Susan and I leaned on a community of supporters to help Alex, we all must recognize the importance of building and accepting support in our lives.

If you're facing a difficult challenge, let this remind you to reach out, seek help, and let others in. And when life gives you the opportunity, be the person who steps in for someone else's storm. Because as much as we need others, others will need us one day. These shared connections and acts of kindness help us endure, heal, and grow stronger. So take your hardships and let them be the fire that fuels you to lift someone else, and in doing so, you'll find your sense of purpose and peace.

These are the moments that make you think about life and what matters. You find yourself reflecting on everything you have ever learned, and, hopefully, you take the positive lessons and pay them forward. That is what I was wired to do; it is why I have worked to help people around me, and it is why, at the time, I decided to search for another venture that could allow me to help others improve their way of thinking and their health and happiness.

For whatever reason, I had been handed so many personal challenges to overcome in my life. A broken household with a father whom I loved but who was abusive to my mother. A mother who was in severe depression during my teenage years, who developed ulcerative colitis and colorectal cancer. Dysfunctional siblings with multiple addictions and significant disabilities. And perhaps the most compelling of all, a severely disabled son and no toolkit or road map to figure out how to manage his journey. These challenges were unbearable and created profound anxiety that disrupted my thinking, my focus, and my sense of discipline at moments throughout my lifetime. And here I was, unemployed, without a deep nest egg, and working through a cataclysmic personal challenge at home. I was mentally and emotionally fried but still convinced I could grind my way through it.

PART II

GROW OR FOLD

At some point in every life, we find ourselves staring into the abyss of a fundamental choice: **Grow or Fold.** It's rarely a neat, convenient moment. More often, it's messy, painful, and disorienting—a life out of balance, personal and professional chaos, a purpose slipped through our fingers without us even noticing. **The chapters ahead chronicle what happens when you make the difficult but powerful decision to grow.**

This is the story of rebuilding from the inside out—personally and professionally—with a renewed sense of purpose. It begins by facing harsh truths without rationalization or excuses. It demands that we take a real inventory of where we are, ask hard questions about what we truly want, and summon the courage to design a new life anchored in health, meaning, and authentic success.

You'll walk through the critical steps that allowed me to turn a midlife crisis into a midlife reinvention: taking stock of my personal and professional worlds, crystallizing a new vision for my future, converting dreams into actionable goals, and clarifying a purpose that could carry me through the most brutal storms.

Grow or Fold is not just a concept—it's a way of living, thinking, and committing to change when the easier choice would be to stay where you are. You'll find practical methods, harsh reflections, and personal insights to guide your journey forward. Because ultimately, life isn't about avoiding struggle. It's about rising through it—and becoming stronger, wiser, and more alive on the other side.

Let's get to work.

CHAPTER SIX

GROW OR FOLD?

There Is Only One Choice

So here we are, back at age fifty, and my life is in disarray on every level. When I stepped back and looked at where I was in 2010, I remember thinking about my challenges from a different perspective. Things were so chaotic and unstable; it was as if I were sitting on a stool with shaky legs that felt like they were about to break. Are you with me? You know that feeling when a chair has a wobbly or loose leg? Well, in this case, my stool had three broken legs:

- Personally: My life was in crisis on every level.
- Professionally: I was out of a job with no clarity on what to do.
- Purpose: I had not clearly defined my mission or reason for being.

So I went to work on myself.

First and foremost, I found some extraordinary specialists who guided me through this critical period. You can't make change happen in a vacuum—we all need people to assist us in essential areas, and mental health is where I started. I found an amazing psychologist named Susan Braiman in New York. Susan specialized in working with parents of children with autism and other disabilities, so she had a unique window into the complex challenges we were facing and tons of experience in helping people navigate it. She also worked with families who were dealing with elder care and addiction, and this was the trifecta that I was struggling with. Lastly, she was wired and connected me with some great MDs who guided me through the myriad of physical challenges that I faced.

The medical challenges I was dealing with were new and confusing to me. I had been diagnosed with metabolic syndrome. Out of nowhere, I was prediabetic, on top of my preexisting hypothyroidism. I also saw a tremendous spike in my cholesterol, and there was no doubt that my blood chemistry was significantly out of balance, contributing to my mental instability. I also learned that all of this was a potential precursor to numerous physical impairments that would lead to disease if I didn't respond quickly. At fifty years old, I was feeling vulnerable in so many ways for the first time in my life. I was sleeping only three to four hours a night and ruminating on all the challenges and fears I was facing. In addition, I knew that if I didn't figure out a way to calm my brain, I would have significant lifelong challenges that would interfere with any possibility of stability and happiness.

Without therapy, I would not be where I am today. I had seen therapists throughout my adult life, but most of them treated me with kid gloves and just scratched the surface of the work I needed to do on myself. This therapist was different: serious and intense but also kind at the same time. She could not be swayed in her resolve to convince me that I needed to make some significant changes if I was going to live a long and healthy life. I was drinking a lot to put out the fire, gorging on unhealthy food, and I was struggling with massive worry and guilt as everyone around me was declining. I was anxious, and my fuse was short because I was grinding so hard emotionally. I felt that I was playing a game I couldn't win.

One day, in the middle of a therapy session, she said something to me that hit at the core of my soul: "Matt, everyone in your world is disabled. You can't get sucked into being everyone's caretaker. Most importantly, your wife needs you, Alex needs you, and Jason needs you. *If you don't make personal changes, you will not be here to help them.*"

IT WAS AS IF THE MUSIC IN THE ROOM STOPPED.

I started crying as I thought about Susan having to battle our challenges at home without me, and Alex and Jason not having me there to help them grow. My father left home when I was a teen and was rarely there to guide me, but *my boys needed my presence, and Susan needed a partner.* It was an unbearable thought for me. At the same time, it was a massive fucking wake-up call. She reframed exactly what I was dealing with and gave me the license to make critical changes in how I related to my family. I felt the shackles of guilt and worry loosening around my soul.

The lifelong guilt I struggled with as I watched my brothers in a constant downward spiral forced me into the fire, and their addictions and dysfunction were sucking the life out of me. This was a pattern over the previous twenty years, but through therapy, I was now being taught how to give tough love, how to create space, how to not fall prey to the manipulation and guilt of others with their disease. I joined Al-Anon and started to build a toolkit to deal with the insidious menace of familial addiction. I learned to let go of the past. She guided me through the crisis that my son was going through. Without a doubt, this was the toughest period of my life and undoubtedly the most difficult personal challenge I had ever faced. I had a beautiful wife and family that I loved, but I was anxious and at times, so impulsive and angry that I couldn't build a sustainable daily routine where I felt calm and happy.

So I started to dig deeper and realized that I needed to make dramatic personal changes if I were going to create long-term success and happiness. When you looked at my skills, I was an extraordinary salesperson, and when you combined my persuasive ability with my intensity to fight, my perseverance, and my strength, I would almost always achieve my intended outcome. *But not this time.* I didn't have a mental disease, but I had massive anxiety and sleep issues. I didn't have any mission-critical diseases, but I was on my way to diabetes, heart disease, and alcoholism. I didn't have social challenges, but there were times when I was too complicated, impulsive, and confrontational. Even though I thought of myself as a lovable, kind, and soft-spoken person, there were moments when I was uncontrollably intense.

THE WORLD DIDN'T KNOW HOW HARD MY WORLD WAS.

And frankly, no one ever knows what others are dealing with. That is, at least in part, why we need to give one another grace. You never know the fight someone is fighting. It could be an insurmountable one. That might be why they are lashing out, short tempered with you, or incapable of building meaningful relationships. We are all so quick to judge the energy of another without truly understanding why people act that way in the first place.

I knew my energy was imbalanced. It was off. I wasn't presenting the way I always did in my own life. Guess what? I was the only one who needed to stare it straight in the face and deal with it. Some basic guideposts started to speak to me loudly:

- I needed to do the work on myself.
- I needed to create a *clear vision* for the kind of person I wanted to be and how I wanted to feel.

- I needed to define exactly what would make me happy ten years later.
- How did I want people to think about me?
- Who did I want to spend my time with?
- How would I develop a plan to manage my challenges at home and avoid succumbing to these overwhelming difficulties?
- Could I outline a new, calmer, more thoughtful, slower-moving, emotionally engaged, and healthier personal side?

As I was migrating through all my challenges, I was also focused on tackling my professional plan. Could this fuel the foundation of a new professional path with a real sense of purpose that would guide me through the second half of my life?

While becoming more enamored with the idea of building a new venture, I went to work on creating a business plan that would help me launch One River School and create a self-sustaining venture. There were no great examples for me, and the business of running an art school didn't seem economically viable. But the idea excited me, and I needed to clarify the *why* first. Why did this business concept fit my values, skills, goals, and needs? It seemed a bit like a new professional path, but it also felt familiar, and I thought that it might perfectly align with a vision that I had for myself.

Here is what I came up with:

1. **I believe art-making = wellness.** *There is great medicinal value in making art.* I saw this firsthand as a little boy by watching my dad paint. I observed the emotional benefits and thought I could help people of all ages with their mental health and wellness via One River while also teaching them to maximize their creative skills.

2. **I'm driven by creative curiosity.** *I am fascinated with what drives creativity.* How people approach achieving creative outcomes is at the top of my passions.
3. **I love to help people grow.** *The developmental benefit of making art is profound for people of all ages.* I lived this every day at School of Rock and at home with my boys, and I wanted to help more people stretch their capacity for growth.
4. **I want to celebrate living artists.** *There are two million living artists in America, and most people couldn't name three!* I became inspired to celebrate living artists and wanted to create context for them by teaching their work and honoring them in the classroom.
5. **I want to create career opportunities in the arts.** *There were so few great career opportunities in the visual arts.* I loved and was good at building teams and creating employee-centric cultures. We could make One River the *best place to work in the arts*™!
6. **I saw a business opportunity.** *"Doing well by doing good" motivated me to the core.* This seemed like a perfect extension of School of Rock—another business opportunity that aligned with an authentic challenge and personal mission. Helping others is what I need in my life for the rest of my life.

This exercise can help you vet new opportunities:

1. Start by writing the question at the top of a page.
   For me it was: **Why should I open an art school?**
2. Next, write down all the reasons *why* you should.
3. Next, anchor those *whys* to the innate skill set you maintain and possess.

This exercise will help you realize not just if it is a good idea, but if it is a good idea for you, and the analysis can help you realize if your goals connect with your skills.

At fifty years old, I realized that, more than anything, I was interested in aligning my professional and personal growth with a venture that would enhance my life's purpose. One River seemed to be the holy grail, and for the first time, I wanted to throw my heart and soul into my idea and build a purely entrepreneurial venture. And that is precisely what I did. As I was working through 2012, I spent almost two years studying everything I could about the contemporary art world and the art education space. With my best preparation, I launched One River School in Englewood, New Jersey, in September 2012. The goal was to create a fun and compelling art-making experience, near my home, for people of all ages. A place for people to learn, grow, and tap into the other side of their brain. This venture was not just about making money; if we were to be successful, this business would be about much more.

Now that I had the critical *why* stuff out of the way, I faced the overwhelming challenge of convincing myself that I wouldn't go broke doing it. How could this make any sense from an investment standpoint?

Here are some of the questions I was facing relative to the business concept:

- Why were there no successful, recreational, for-profit art schools in America?
- Why were there no cool places to make art in suburbia?
- Why was art education broken in America?
- Was there an opportunity to fix it?
- Why was art education stuck in the past?
- How come so few people understood contemporary art?
- How come almost no one could name three living artists?
- Could I quickly self-educate and become an expert?
- Could I build a school that was fun, cool, and relevant?

- Could I create a *new method of art education* where the educational results were great?
- And the business model worked?

If I were going to succeed, it was crucial to evaluate each question above. So, whenever you take on a new role, opportunity, or investment or determine which direction to head, asking thought-provoking questions can make a substantial difference in how you build strategy. These questions would help me navigate numerous potential challenges by determining all the layers and complexity I was going to face.

Frankly, it wasn't logical for anyone to tell me it would be a good business investment. I couldn't find one successful for-profit art school anywhere! I had no reference point to benchmark success. Almost every venture in the space was a nonprofit, and nearly all of them suffered from low funding, operational losses, uninspired studios, unsophisticated marketing, and various indicators that told me an art school may be a disastrous economic idea. However, I knew that the concept I had in mind perfectly fit my value system. In addition, I was so curious and inspired by contemporary art that I started to collect artwork made by unproven, emerging contemporary artists. Then something extraordinary happened. The more I collected art, the more inspired I became. This led me to throw my whole body into self-education, and the more I read and studied, the more passionate I became about contemporary art.

What drove these artists to make weird, idiosyncratic artwork? What drove their decisions? What was the arc of their art practice and how had they evolved? I wanted to share their stories with others to learn more about art and potentially develop a new passion for the art of today. Most people have never engaged with contemporary art, and few regularly practice making art. My mission was to change this, centered on the idea of *teaching through the lens of living artists*™.

There was another important factor that pushed me over the fence. I had real-world experience building an early-stage creative education venture into a widely distributed, successful brand. Five years of grinding to build School of Rock was graduate school in scaling a multi-unit concept. But School of Rock was so much easier than One River; it had such a simple and obvious magic recipe. Teach kids rock and roll and put them on stages to perform. It was sticky, and the emotional payoff was gigantic. The brand had implied magic from the wildly successful movie with Jack Black. Music education was highly valued in parents' minds, and we had a unique product in the market. Lastly, a super cool viral tool allowed us to get massive press and promotion. Rock stars came to play with our students, and we were good at cultivating them and their interest in us.

So, for One River to be successful, I would have to invent a product and delivery model, build a curriculum, design a space, build a brand, hire and motivate a team, and raise capital. This massive challenge drove me. Problem-solving and strategy fueled a creative outlet for me, and I was encouraged to build something new from my heart and soul.

Here's how I looked at the venture from a micro perspective. The first step was to build something innovative and accessible and get people to try us. Once they tried us, the task was on One River to make it fun and compelling. If we could achieve that goal, people would stay with us, we would make a difference in their lives, and we would build something that otherwise didn't exist in the marketplace. One River could ultimately become a place to channel my energy in a way that would align with my life goals and professional goals as I moved more deeply into middle age.

So, at the beginning of 2012, Scott McGraw and I put some money into getting the business going. I found a location in Englewood, New Jersey, signed a lease, hired a construction firm, and set September 2012 for our grand opening. Matt Boskin, one of the greatest people I know and one of my best friends, who was also an early investor in School of Rock, stepped up and wrote a check to back me. I am so grateful to him as a friend and as an invaluable shoulder to lean on through all that I was dealing with. And he believed in me and has always been there when I needed help and support while dealing with the challenges of early-stage businesses and life. Paul Spitzberg, another friend and exceptional human being, was right there with a check as well.

I had begun the journey and was fully committed to building something special for the community. The easy part was pulling the rip cord and deciding to do it; the hard part would be executing and creating a highly polished experience valued by our consumers. Despite everything you hear about overnight success stories, 99.99 percent are inaccurate. From fall 2012 through the end of 2014, we were doing a nice job, but we were unclear about how to provide a consistently replicable experience. And no matter what, I was not prepared to open more locations if I couldn't convince myself that we could be amazing at operating and execution, finding the right talent to work for us, building a marketing model that allowed us to create traction, and enrolling enough people to pay our bills and generate some positive cash flow.

I'm happy to say that we figured it out. With the extraordinary talent and effort of Agnes Mauro and Angela Shin behind it, our Englewood location turned into a phenomenal success that became the prototype that fueled our motivation to grow. From 2017 to 2019, we grew from one to fourteen locations, provided a service to thousands of students, differentiated ourselves in the market, and built something that has tremendous scalable potential to this day. During the COVID window, I decided to slow down unit growth and tighten our experience while preserving capital to support our future initiatives. Today, the business is on a very successful foundation with fifteen schools in six states, we have a team that is passionate about what we do, and maybe most exciting of all, we have built a company that I believe is *the best place to work in the arts*™.

To recap, in 2010, *all three legs of the stool of my life were broken*: Professionally, I was out of a job; personally, my life was in crisis; and I had not clarified a specific purpose that would govern how I behaved in the future. But as I sit here today and reflect on that moment, I couldn't be prouder of my work to establish what drove my happiness, health, success, and purpose. And I put a plan in place to continue to drive my growth. It took a decade or more for me to retrain my brain on how to think and behave daily. And the work continues every day of my life. Excellence and happiness are not a given for anyone, but there is an approach that can be tailor-made to the skills, traits, goals, and personal styles of each of us.

Over the balance of this book, I will share the detailed methods that allowed me to Grow rather than Fold in the face of adversity and a dramatic series of challenges. As part of this, I will also provide a thoughtful and systematic way to evaluate where you are, where you want to get to, the gaps and challenges that are in the way, and a plan to do the work to transform your life.

CHAPTER SEVEN

THE WORK BEGINS

It Starts with Taking Inventory

We experience and navigate the same process, whether focusing on creating wholesale change or just fine-tuning a few aspects of our lives. It requires time, focus, and a step-by-step system. And, in many ways, it's the same process whether you are fixing a business or trying to solve personal challenges impacting your life.

In 2010, I had a massive amount of work to do, given the complexity of the challenges I was facing both personally and professionally. So I sat down to build a road map that would allow me to deeply analyze where I was, where I wanted to get to, and how I was going to get there. This road map was like a functional GPS, and it helped me commit to staying on course and not being judgmental about the time it was going to take to get to the destination.

For the record, I am not sure that I know one person who didn't struggle at some time with trying to understand what drove their happiness during middle age.

Here is a sample list of what many of us find ourselves navigating:

- Do you need to make profound changes in your professional life?
- Do have to overcome challenges at home?
- Are you struggling with how to improve your health?
- Are you trying to quiet the noise in your head?
- Maybe you don't feel inspired or connected to a cause.
- Or there's a general uncertainty of where life is taking you.
- Maybe you are stuck in a relationship—personal or professional—that is not providing the positive outcomes that you are looking for and deserve.
- Or are you dealing with some health issues that are new to you?
- Elderly parents?
- Concerns about finances?
- Stressed out?

I had them all! And more!

Even though I was a tremendous success to the outside world, at fifty, I was overwhelmed, and every aspect of my life was in a nosedive.

Right now, you may have countless things creating profound concerns and worry. That's where I was. However, after significant soul searching, I started to clarify the broader challenge and figure out some things that laid the groundwork to transform my life. That work, which we will do together, will help you to unravel your challenges and allow you to develop a plan to reset yourself.

TAKING INVENTORY

The three-legged stool of growth: **Personal. Professional. Purpose.**

If you think about the metaphor of a three-legged stool, it's simple: A stool with a broken leg will fall to the ground. Back in 2010, I had three broken legs and no clarity on how to put the stool back together. We all have a different series of challenges and capabilities, but no matter how you slice it, facing those challenges starts with taking a deep inventory to determine where you are so that you can decode what is working and what is not.

To that end, let's analyze each of the three legs of our lives—personal, professional, and purpose—to identify which specific areas will require a focused effort to reset ourselves and move to a different place over the next decade. This is going to require some real self-searching because most people are stuck doing things the way they have always done them, and we must tackle this demon head-on, or there is no simple pathway to grow or change.

THE DYSFUNCTIONAL SAFE ZONE™

Before we jump in, I want to spend a minute sharing some thoughts about this concept. Having coached hundreds of professionals during my career, I have often been amazed by the natural tendency to rationalize behavior and accept the status quo, even though it may lead to a downward performance over time. This same adverse tendency is omnipresent in how we manage our personal lives, and this gets in the way of making required changes to generate new outcomes.

Rationalization is ingrained in our brains, and it often serves a great purpose. It's a coping tool that allows us to work through difficult things and prevents us from being too hard on ourselves. But this behavior interferes with our ability to shift gears. As a result, we wind up getting stuck in a suboptimal recurring cycle. We will have to be aware of and manage this self-limiting behavior, or we will not work decisively to make critical shifts in our execution.

We are about to jump in and start to do some of the most important work in our lives.

NOTE: I put months into this process, and I want to be clear about this up front. I also want to do all that I can to make the process of reading this book AND doing the workflow as effective as possible. So, throughout the areas in the book where there are assignments that require time, effort, brainstorming, and a chance to process important information in a thoughtful way, I have included tools that you can also use for free at my website MattRoss.com.

If you want to read the book and come back to the workflow, look for the highlighted areas with QR codes and links.

My only goal is to guide you through this at the pace that works best for you. Lastly, to make this more tangible, I am going to work side by side with you and share my personal workflow to create a reference point for each exercise.

So, take a deep breath, and let's begin to think about what's working and not working in *your personal life.*

To do so, start by thinking about some basic questions:

- How are your relationships with your family and significant others?
- How are your relationships with friends?
- How is your physical health?
- How is your mental health?
- How is your motivation to learn and grow?
- How is your energy?
- How is your confidence?

Try and set your rationalization to the side. It is easy to find a way to explain to yourself that "it's all good." But *it is in your own best interest to identify what you want to improve in your personal life.* It is that simple. How you score yourself will determine how you build a plan to improve and enhance your quality of life. and that is something that we are going to work on next.

PERSONAL INVENTORY

Let's take your **personal inventory.**

Answer the following questions on a scale of 1–10 with 10 being the highest score you can give yourself. The questions are broken into four clusters of three questions each that allow a self-appraisal in the following areas: social, health, motivation, and general state of mind.

1	How happy are you with your life today?	_____(G)
2	Do you have at least five close personal friends?	_____(S)
3	How would you rate your overall current health?	_____(H)
4	Do you have specific goals for the next three and five years?	_____(M)
5	Is your energy level great?	_____(H)
6	Are you confident in your ability to create change?	_____(M)
7	Do you seek out social situations rather than being alone?	_____(S)
8	Do you have a very clear health and wellness program in place?	_____(H)
9	Is your support system fantastic?	_____(S)
10	Do you generally wake up excited about the day ahead?	_____(M)

11	Do you generally feel at ease and content?	____(G)
12	Do you feel happy and excited about your future prospects?	____(G)
Total up your current personal inventory score: ____		

Now that you've totaled your score, let's dig deeper to understand some trends and better diagnose where you need to focus your efforts. You could have scored a maximum of 120 on this survey. I scored 35 out of 120 when I did this. That was a jarring 30 percent of the highest possible score. Now, I knew 120 was unrealistic, but I thought I could crack 100. My score confirmed that I was really struggling, but it didn't give me all the information I needed. Specifically, what aspects of my personal life were least functional?

When I dug deeper, I realized that I scored 15 out of 30 in the **social** category. That meant that I scored 50 percent, but I felt that my social gaps were a function of my other critical deficiencies because I was in such a bad state of mind. *I scored 20 out of 84 when I eliminated social* and studied the three other categories, which put me at less than 25 percent of the max and clearly told me that I was broken.

I scored an 8 out of 30 on both my **health** and **general state of being.** Less than 30 percent for each. This was eye opening. When I dug even deeper, I realized that my **motivation** score was a 4 out of 30! Middle age brought me to this, but I was also going through massive upheaval: my disabled son's psychiatric breakdown, my parents' declining health, my brother's profound mental disease, and the loss of a job. These were barriers to my motivation, health, and happiness.

So, let's look at how you scored yourself across all these specific categories. We can then focus on which areas of your personal life need to be reinvented. Afterward, I will help you create a deeper thought process around how to spend your time to improve the essential areas of your life that are broken or simply need a reset.

Total your score by category:

CATEGORY	QUESTION #	CUMULATIVE SCORE
Social	2, 7, & 9	
Health	3, 5, & 8	
Motivation	4, 6, & 10	
General	1, 11, & 12	

Once we complete our inventory across all three legs of the stool, we will dig into each of these categories over the next three chapters to further analyze where we are and work on strategies to put a comprehensive plan in place.

PROFESSIONAL INVENTORY

At some point in our lives, we find ourselves deeply rooted in a career path but experience low job and career satisfaction. That's because in the early stages of our careers, we were hardwired to learn and grow and likely became committed to an industry and a professional space that made sense with our developing adult sensibility. We put our foot on the gas and focused on creating financial stability while possibly supporting the development of a family. Predictability was often a massive requirement.

If you are thriving in your career, highly engaged, and certain about what you want to do for the next twenty years, then you are lucky and rare. If this is the case, you can move on to the next section. But for most people in the middle of their life, our jobs are how we spend the bulk of our time, and research tells us that most of us have work to do to figure out how to maximize our professional pathway.

Let's take your **professional inventory.**

On a scale of 1–10 with 10 high:

1	How happy are you with your current role and company?	
2	Do you receive quality support and coaching from your supervisor?	
3	Do you spend most of your time working on the things you do best?	
4	Do you spend most of your time on things you love to do the most?	
5	Are there significant opportunities to learn in your current role?	
6	Are you compensated in a manner that you feel good about?	
7	Are you happy with your overall career today?	
8	Do you feel certain you are on the right career path for the future?	
9	Do you rarely think about switching jobs or careers?	
10	Do you have many alternate paths available to you?	
11	Do you have great ability to take on new career risk?	
12	Do you derive great joy from what you do for a living?	
Total up your current personal inventory score:		

You could have scored a maximum of 120 in this section. The first six questions are a self-appraisal of your current job, and the next six questions are a self-appraisal of where you are relative to your career ambition. Evaluate your score in the two specific categories that define your professional inventory:

CATEGORY	QUESTION #	CUMULATIVE SCORE
Job	1-6	
Career	7-12	

I had a very difficult time answering some questions on my first attempt and scored under 20 percent of the maximum total. Even though I was unemployed, I wasn't in a financial free fall. Owning School of Rock franchises provided me with some professional engagement and current income, which also gave me time to work on myself.

In 2011, I found some consulting projects to keep me busy, but I felt uncertain about whether I wanted to go back to work in another corporate setting. I went from building and being at the center of a very significant business to feeling isolated and without a team to engage with. And I had no immediate solution for how I was going to transition my career. So much of my self-worth and status was tied to my professional achievements, and this was clearly having an impact on my health and well-being.

What does your score tell you?

- Are you in the right company doing the right things?
- Is there an opportunity to grow and change within the firm?
- Do you need to look outside of your company to get what you're looking for?

- Perhaps it's bigger than that?
- Has the industry around you changed in a way that gives you less satisfaction or confidence that you can maximize your professional opportunities?
- Are there other things that you've always dreamed about doing?

For each of these two categories, you should score somewhere north of 50 out of 60, or better than 85 percent, to continue what you're doing and not focus on pivoting. It is challenging to make a significant change in your professional trajectory; it requires work and thoughtful planning. We're going to spend a chapter dedicated to this, and I'm going to share some tricks that hopefully will help you optimize how you focus on your professional future.

But before we do, let's move on to what might be the most important piece, which also has a correlation with your professional path. Do you have a real sense of real purpose? Do you even know what that looks and feels like?

PURPOSE INVENTORY

So now that we have done some work to baseline our current personal and professional state, let's look at the next item: your passion. This inventory is going to be different. We are not going to focus on a grading system. It will be more contextual in how we think through this. There are some big questions to ask and some important things for you to think about, which can dramatically influence your happiness for the rest of your life. Before we go there, I want to share a bit more context.

Stephen Covey changed my life. His book *The 7 Habits of Highly Effective People* framed a basic toolkit that I have leaned on for the past thirty years. The second habit, "Begin with the end in mind," speaks clearly to this topic. Here's what Stephen says:

> If you don't make a conscious effort to visualize who you are and what you want in life, then you empower other people and circumstances to shape you and your life by default. It's about connecting again with your uniqueness and then defining the personal, moral, and ethical guidelines within which you can most happily express and fulfill yourself.[2]

Over the course of our lives, it is easy for us to get further and further away from what motivates us most. In general, I have always tried to put my head down and grind my way through life, relying on my instincts, talent, planning, and effort. I went to work; I listened to my gut. I studied, worked hard, moved fast, made mistakes, and invested in trying to squeeze as much joy out of my job, my family, my friends, and my life as I could. It often meant that I had strong opinions about who I was, and if things weren't working out, I would simply push harder and persevere. I was blessed with tremendous stamina and intensity and leaned on these traits for the first thirty years of my career and adult life.

But, as you recall, at fifty years old I reflected on a book called *What Got You Here Won't Get You There*. I loved the metaphor in general, and it forced me to come to terms with this:

> If I was going to be happier and healthier, more focused and less anxious, more disciplined and more productive, more financially successful, and a better person for my family, this was the time for me to think more deeply about the meaning of life and my unique qualities, skills, interests, and motivations:
>
> - Could I align myself with something new where I would be able to generate more happiness?
> - Were there things that would bring me more joy and more emotional engagement?
> - Did I even know what made me feel most fulfilled?

- Could I do more to help others and learn more about myself in the process?
- Could I find a new career path that would align my personal mission and purpose while also maximizing my economic opportunities and my professional skill set?

Let's take your **purpose inventory.**

We have a writing exercise that is going to prove to be incredibly important. So get out your computer or grab a piece of paper and take some time to respond to the following questions/statements in two simple sentences for each item:

1. I am passionate about these things:
2. If I could do anything with my daily time, what would I do?
3. What "special powers" do I have that make me unique?
4. I get really excited when I think about this:
5. What two things would I like to contribute to society?
6. I would love to help people in the following ways:
7. My passion often has me thinking about this:
8. If I had to describe myself in *two words*, what would they be?
9. I simply feel great when I spend time doing this:
10. I would feel most fulfilled if I can help people in this way:

This is a brainstorming exercise, and there are no right or wrong answers. However, I find that the first things that pop into your head are often closest to the right answers for you. It may take time, and you might need to revisit it more than once. But take the time to make a list and come back to it if you are not clear. I want you to have definitive answers to these questions if we are going to help you move forward and grow. This exercise should help you anchor what makes you most *excited*, *motivated*, and *driven to live*. There is no formula; we are all unique, and we all have an individualized sense of what motivates and excites us.

However, there is one thing we all share: We are all bound by the law of limited time. How you allocate your time today, tomorrow, and for the rest of your life is a choice. Again, we will come back to this in a dedicated chapter that will give us more time to focus on creating a clear sensibility around what drives our purpose.

INVENTORY ROLLUP

In this chapter, we began the important work that will now guide us as we move through the rest of the book. It was essential to look at each of the three legs of the stool that contribute to our happiness and quality of life. Remember, we have developed deeply rooted habits that are hard to break in middle age, and lots of them are built for the right reasons. But at the same time, we continue to rely on a lot of habits that are no longer helpful, and if you don't take the time to carefully reflect on where you are, what is working, and what is not working, it is virtually impossible to make significant progress toward improving your quality of life.

Over the next few chapters, we are going to dig deeper to **evaluate the components of our lives that govern our health, wealth, and sense of self.** Now that we've begun to analyze our personal and professional lives and think about identifying a real purpose to galvanize our spirit, we will crystallize the areas that we want to work on and deploy a program to drive change. This work is among the most important work you will do in your lifetime. The gap between fair and good is small. The gap between good and great is gigantic. But here is an essential point:

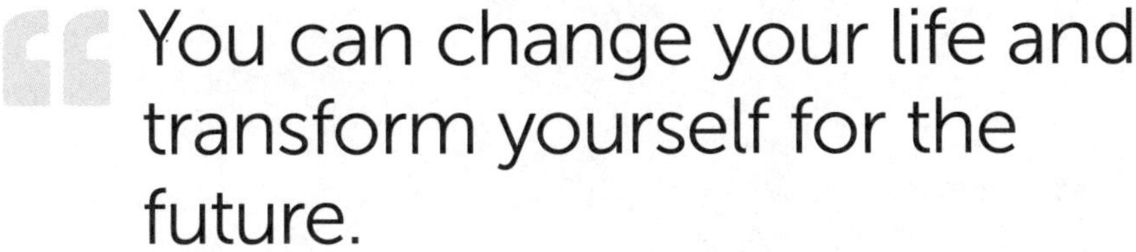

And, as you begin to do the work, I will also continue to share some anecdotes about the work I did, the bumps in the road, and the learnings that I uncovered along the way.

Scan QR code for the downloadable or digital version of the assignment:

TAKING INVENTORY
Personal • Professional • Purpose

CHAPTER EIGHT

CREATING PERSONAL CHANGE

What's Your Vision?

At the ripe age of fifty years old, I became deeply aware that my toolkit wasn't going to get the job done. I knew I needed a more thoughtful approach to managing my personal life, and I had to find a new method to guide me, or I had to build a new framework that would allow me to transcend the uncertainty and challenges I faced. The fact is that I was stuck, and life became hard on such a complex scale. We all have these moments—the fateful ones where we feel like we have nowhere to go and are unsure of the path ahead or wonder if we can even find the strength to put one foot in front of the other.

Let's be clear. These moments are all relative, and I am aware that many people are fighting their way through even more significant and grave challenges, with fewer resources and skills, compared to what I was dealing with. However, no matter the case or the circumstances, here are the core ideas that I want you to think about:

- The goal for all of us is to strip down our vanity and ego so that they fade into the background.
- This book is about work, investment in learning, and belief in our ability to overcome obstacles.
- These elements are at the root of creating personal change.

And none of it would've happened for me if I didn't have the conviction to focus on a future destination for which I was searching—I simply would not settle for anything less.

It is also important to note that the task of repositioning yourself at any time shouldn't come at the expense of diminishing the hard work and accomplishments that you have achieved on your journey. I built a practice of deep commitment to personal growth throughout my life, creating a solid foundation to build on. I have been a lifelong learner, earned a master's degree, and spent a disproportionate amount of my time reading, exploring, and challenging the notion of what drives excellence. So, despite the lifetime grind I was going through, I was constantly working on getting my head into a positive space by reflecting on my journey and my growth along the way.

Now, as you begin to work on what is not working and what you need to change, *it is massively important for you to get your head into a positive space.*

We understand the concept of optimizing your mental performance in athletic endeavors, but it is easily as important for creating the mental framework to overcome our greatest personal challenges. In fact, the process is cathartic, and there is also a scientific reason I am recommending this. You will enhance the quality of your work by stimulating a variety of brain chemicals at the onset of this work via taking some time to reflect on your most joyful and successful moments.

SO HERE'S A FANTASTIC WARM-UP TO GET YOU IN THE RIGHT FRAME OF MIND.

I want you to write a couple of paragraphs or more that *highlight important positive/successful milestones that you achieved in your life*. Here are mine:

I found a wife in Susan, whom I love, care for, and will grow old with. We have raised two children, Alex and Jason, who bring us so much joy, notwithstanding the challenges we have faced with Alex's disabilities. I have many wonderful friends, and my career up until the age of fifty has been mostly what I wanted, even with the obstacles I faced.

Along the way, I achieved great professional goals as the CEO of School of Rock and during my career in media, where I was responsible for building and operating some of the most important radio properties in the country, including Q104.3, New York's classic rock station.

The radio industry of the '80s and '90s was a unique and formative place for me, and I squeezed out some of the most special experiences that I could during my time. We broke the most important music of our era while building great brands and helping thousands of advertisers achieve their marketing goals. I was also fortunate to take clients on trips all over the world. I attended the opening ceremony and numerous events of the 1996 Olympics. I've been to the World Series, Super Bowls . . . you name it. My passion for music was paramount, and I saw every great band in the world, met many of my idols, and could share countless stories. I even got to stand onstage with the Who at Madison Square Garden in 2000!

In 2001, I was an executive producer for Summer Jam, one of the largest hip-hop concert events in the world, held at Giants Stadium, and turned it into a TV special. Along the way, I helped to produce and manage hundreds of other events that were special to me. One of the things I am most proud of is the creation of the Q104 Kids Foundation. Bob Buchmann, my morning host and program director, helped me to develop this concept, and we raised millions of dollars to fund early intervention services for kids with autism.

> As Founder of One River School, I am now focused on continuing to grow and carve out a unique niche in the creative education space. We are working hard to *transform art education®*, while also becoming *the best place to work in the arts™*. Every day I have a unique view into the extraordinary growth and joy our students and teammates derive from what we do.

That felt so good!

Now, I want you to do the same thing. Keep the following in mind:

- This is a brainstorming warm-up.
- You deserve it, and the task of reflecting on your accomplishments will generate the right energy to focus on the work we are about to jump into.
- Write freely and get that smile on your face by documenting some moments that are lifetime highlights.

GO!

VISION

What comes to mind when you hear the word *vision*? If you are super literal, the first thing that might pop into your head is your basic sense of sight. That is a traditional definition of the word and a good place to start. When it comes to life planning, business building, or trying to create substantial change, this word takes on a slightly different meaning.

According to the *Oxford Dictionary*, vision is also "the ability to think about or plan the future with imagination or wisdom." In this definition, let's focus on the most important elements: "imagination or wisdom." When it comes to planning your personal future, I want to correct the brilliant people at Oxford because *or* should be *and*—you must have both!

> Vision = the ability to think about or plan the future with imagination AND wisdom.

Having a dream is one part of this, but you will struggle without a thoughtful plan to achieve your outcome. So, with that said, let's go to work on clarifying our vision, and let's start by looking at the personal inventory we worked on in the last chapter. It's helpful to step back and look at your results again to evaluate your current state. Think about what you want to change, prioritizing what's most important. For instance, having the beautiful vacation home at the beach might sound like a great personal goal, but it may not be achievable in the near term.

To help accomplish this, **take a look at the four categories we discussed in your personal inventory** that we completed and put them in order from lowest score to highest score.

As you can recall, I prioritized my health issues, both physical and mental, which impacted everything else in my life. I was dealing with massive external factors, but I had compelling personal challenges that I *had to address first*. As a result, it was easy for me to sit and do the work of documenting what was broken and what I needed to fix. Now that you are focusing on what you want to improve, let's start to articulate it.

TIPS

The way that I start this is I open the Notes app on my iPhone and begin speaking into my phone to document my thoughts. Or I open a document on my computer and dictate. For some reason, I feel a greater emotional connection when I hear myself saying the things I want to achieve out loud. At this point, I'm not editing. I'm just thinking and speaking out loud to document my dreams and wishes.

Communicating the life that you want to lead out loud also creates a metaphysical response: When you hear yourself, you reinforce the importance of what you are saying. The information travels from your lips to your ears to your heart and to your head. It is a powerful process that taps into your imagination and wisdom and generates chemicals in your brain and body that are motivating.

This process is iterative and takes time. Make sure your thoughts are speaking from both your heart and mind. And **be patient.** Some of us are blessed with the ability to let this flow and others get stuck. That's okay. Just recognize who you are and find a workaround that allows you to share in a way that works for you.

This exercise should take a contextual approach. It is both important and hard to do at the same time. That's why most of us don't do it. It's easier to stay where you are and to live in the *dysfunctional safe zone*™, to bitch and complain and blame others.

After I started working on this for a little while on my phone, I copied and pasted it and emailed it to myself. After transferring it to a Word or Google Doc, I added to the work and edited it so that it became more structured and orderly.

CRYSTALLIZE YOUR DREAM

Don't you think it's important to know exactly where you are headed? This is one of the key attributes for maximizing your personal happiness. But can you clearly articulate it? I couldn't at first, but when I got deep into this process, I realized that there were clearly things that were in the way that needed to be solved. I also was so busy throughout the first half of midlife that I simply hadn't taken the time to clearly articulate what I wanted most out of life when my kids were grown and I had more time on my hands.

Here are the critical steps to follow:

1. Write a page or two of bullet-point items that articulate *exactly what you want your life to look like in five or ten years*. The truth is, we have lots of time ahead and *clearly defining what you want your life to look like* is paramount to creating a plan to get there.
2. Once completed, share it with more than one person you trust and have them ask questions about your vision. This dialogue will allow you to challenge your assumptions.
3. Did you miss things?
4. Did you identify things that are not practical, or reality based?
5. Do you need to adjust?

MY VISION PLAN: MVP-10™

The next step is to refine the work we just did and get ultra specific around the destination that we are striving for. I sat down to write *my vision plan*, and it was daunting, but as I got into the flow and worked at it, I challenged myself to come up with *ten specific statements* that would inform my goals and allow me to crystallize my dreams.

From this exercise, I turned dreams into a concept called **MVP-10™**, which was the framework that I needed to maximize my happiness in midlife and beyond. Let me share what mine looked like, and hopefully, the results will stimulate some ideas and make the process easier for you to frame.

MATT ROSS MVP-10™ (2011–2012)

1. **I want to create long-term solutions to successfully manage my son's disability.**

   Alex needs lifelong care, and if I manufacture the right plan, I will have taken care of the most complex challenge that I face.

2. **I must prioritize my health and wellness.**

   This starts with *addressing the metabolic syndrome* that I've developed to avoid diabetes. I want to enhance my lifespan by *avoiding the neurodegenerative diseases* Alzheimer's and Parkinson's that run in my family.

3. **I have to do consistent daily work to improve my mental health.**

   It starts with *overcoming a lifetime of guilt and worry* and *reducing my anxiety*. This requires me to make this work *part of my daily life practice*. I can't stop doing the work as soon as I feel good. This muscle will provide the strength I need to manage my parents' decline, my son's disability, my siblings' addictions, and my professional uncertainty and reinforce my toolkit for dealing with new obstacles as I age.

4. **I want to continue to be a great husband and father.**

   My family comes first, and I have to make sure I am available, engaged, supportive, and doing my best at all times.

5. **I need to find a new career track.**

   At this stage of my life, I will *lean in on my passion* to *help people grow* and *become more creative*. My future career track must allow me to *control my own destiny*; I can no longer work for others, and I need to have the *autonomy* to drive the direction of any endeavor that I'm involved with.

6. **In ten years, I want to be unencumbered and have financial abundance.**

   Thoughtful financial planning and diversifying my investment strategy are essential if I am going to *exceed my retirement goals* and give Susan and me the freedom to do the things we have always dreamed of doing, *without worrying about money* as we age.

7. **I want to help others via mentoring and financial support.**

   I will continue to help young executives build their best professional toolkit. In addition, I will provide support to organizations *serving people with autism* and organizations *supporting the arts*. Also, I strive to *become a patron* to help contemporary artists by *building a robust art collection.*

8. **I must continue to invest in my intellectual growth.**

   Lifelong learning is the essence of life, and it will help me enhance my capacity to live long and vibrantly, manage obstacles, and avoid getting stuck in the *dysfunctional safe zone*™.

9. **I want to follow my passion for creativity.**

   I will invest my time and effort into *personal creative projects* and share them with the world while growing and generating *dynamic personal growth* in the process.

10. **I will always strive to do my best.**

    Enough said ☺.

It was cathartic to see these words on paper as goals I wanted to establish for myself. Without having clarity about where I wanted to go, I would have had no logical way to build a thoughtful plan to operate daily.

CREATING YOUR MVP-10™ IS A MUST!

Here's why it matters:

- This process will help you align your personal goals, establish direction for your professional goals, and tap into some nuances that govern your true purpose.
- It creates clarity and guides your future direction, setting in motion the greatest likelihood of long-term happiness and health.
- You will think and behave differently about your future and hopefully better understand the elusive purpose we all search for.

NOTE: While this is a cathartic exercise, the final draft doesn't happen overnight. I really worked on this and edited it four or five times after I knocked out the initial draft. Each time I edited it, I made sure I didn't come back to it for a bunch of days, and I let it sit and marinate. It was empowering to know I could change it at any time I wanted. And I felt a sense of calm as I began to align my future in the direction that offers the greatest likelihood of happiness and health.

Also notice that I defined my health and mental health as the greatest personal challenge I faced, but my first vision item was focused on solutions for my son's challenges. That's because the two were inextricably linked. If I didn't create a plan to care for Alex during and after our lifetime, Susan and I would never have any peace of mind. We knew that Alex couldn't live at home as we aged; we simply couldn't care for him. Therefore, getting the right plan in place and advocating for the right resources and the right professionals to help us help him was essential to finding personal peace and happiness.

There is a sequencing to achieving your vision. It requires you to be logical and practical about how you evolve, while you solve the most compelling challenges you face. To do this we need to be more specific about the intended outcomes we want to achieve, which means *we must refine our vision into goals that allow us to have more details in place.*

Once you have spent some real time and effort documenting the array of items that will allow you to visualize what is most important through your MVP-10™, let's move forward and focus on getting stuff done.

REMEMBER TO USE THE FREE TOOLS AT MATTROSS.COM

Scan QR code for downloadable or digital versions of all *Grow or Fold* assignments

GOALS DRIVE PROGRESS

Maybe you have heard of SMART goals. This is the simplest method for making sure your vision plan gets converted into an action plan. SMART goals are

- specific
- measurable
- achievable
- relevant
- time-bound

Here's how to adopt this simple method for refining your vision into a goal that is rooted in achievable logic. For example, as I tried to solve my most urgent and important MVP-10™ item—"I want to create long-term solutions to manage my son's disability"—I was now ready to clarify the goal with sub-goals that created more specific hurdles for me:

- I need to make sure that Alex is accepted into a residential school so that when he comes out of his crisis, we will have a compelling place for him to live and learn while keeping him safe.
- In five years, at age twenty-two, he will need to be in a home for adults with developmental disabilities.
- We need to find an organization with best-in-class professionals who will care for him, care about him, and are willing to do the gritty and intense daily work to help us keep our boy out of crisis and develop a life plan to manage him.

The clock was ticking. And as Stephen Covey taught me, we needed to "focus on what was urgent and important."[3] We had to manufacture a plan and execute on it. This was priority one and was achievable with hard work and discipline.

MVP item number one was converted into a **SMART goal,** and I was excited to tackle this challenge head-on!

> Life is fucking hard, but living a miserable life, stuck in the same place, with no plan to close the gap, is torturous.
>
> —MATT ROSS

CONVERTING YOUR VISION INTO SMART GOALS

Take the following steps:

- Begin working on the MVP-10™ assignment.
- Take a week or two. Or a month. Or more.
- DO IT!
- After you have gotten comfortable with it, the next step is to convert your vision into specific, time-bound, and achievable goals.

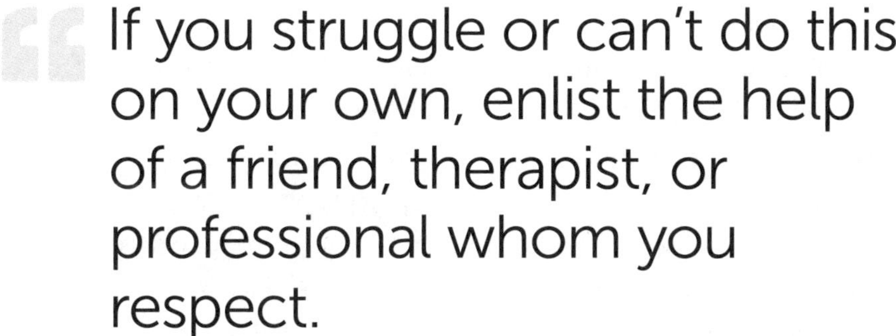

Once you have crystallized your vision/dreams, we must make sure you have a plan to get there. That is where the SMART goals come into play. It is part of being accountable. You can't simply talk about your vision. *You need to get specific about what you want to accomplish and by what date, or it will be almost impossible to put a detailed plan in place.* None of this means that we will seamlessly achieve our transformation. Some things may come easy, and others may be hard, but I assure you that you will have a new sense of pride and appreciation for yourself, and you will feel much more empowered as you evolve by getting busy on the work.

GOALS DEFINE STRATEGY

After you articulate your goals, you need to create a detailed, step-by-step plan to keep you on course.

- What are the steps?
- Over what period of time?
- Who in your life can help you execute?
- Is there a current team to lean on—family, friends, professional resources, etc.?
- What new resources do you need to enlist?

The notion of reaching out, asking for help, and seeking counsel is so often overlooked when it comes to focusing on things that are personal and emotional. Too often, we put our heads down in isolation, and our outcomes are limited by our personal capacity to excel and our ability to step outside ourselves to unemotionally build a plan and solve problems. We simply can't achieve our maximum results without inviting people into the process. While I have exceptional strategic skills, if I didn't invite people into this process, I would not have had the success that I've had. The challenge is not always so obvious. It also requires you to get your ego in check. From my perspective, a lack of self-awareness and proper self-appraisals often determine the difference between success and failure. But it is hard to do.

Let's summarize the steps in this chapter:

1. Crystallize your dream.
2. Create your vision plan: MVP-10™.
3. Convert your vision plan into SMART goals.
4. Refine goals into an action plan.
5. Identify and work with your team to maximize success.

This process is iterative and will take time and passionate effort. But the potential payoff is massive, and it should consume months of work to produce something you can live by. It will allow you to reinvent yourself and change your path for decades to come.

Let's now move on to looking at your professional inventory and enhancing your pathway to success.

Scan QR code for the downloadable or digital version of the assignment: **MVP-10™** **Vision Plan**	

CHAPTER NINE

YOUR PROFESSIONAL PATH

. . . What's Your Magic?

Armed with clarity around your vision, you can begin to drill down on the next steps in your professional journey. You might find yourself at a crossroads, or at least a point where you need to decide between two paths. These paths may take you in very different directions, and that's why it is crucial to determine the right route for you. I had to make that decision when I left the media business and joined School of Rock at a fragile, early stage. Then, after leaving School of Rock, I faced yet another monumental choice. Luckily, I was familiar with the challenge I would soon face, and I knew I had the tools to make the best decision for me and my life. Even so, I knew I had to carefully plot this out. But how? That's where *magic* set in.

If you told me earlier in my life that I would spend twenty years in the media business and then pivot to running a music school, I would've said you're crazy. And if you told me after that, I would build and operate a network of art schools, there would have been zero probability that this would be the trajectory of my career. The fact of the matter is I had built my professional toolkit in the media business, and, as mentioned earlier, it would have made the most sense to continue that journey into digital media. The internet was blossoming in the early 2000s, and almost all my peers were taking leadership roles at early-stage ventures like Google, Spotify, Pandora, and other similar organizations. At the ripe ol' age of forty-five, I had set myself up to optimize my earnings by going deeper into the media business.

However, something was gnawing at me: *I wasn't growing intellectually, and I was only modestly developing on a personal level.*

After twenty years of spending a significant amount of my time focused on generating advertising revenue, I simply didn't want to be doing the same type of deals for the next twenty years. So, when the School of Rock opportunity came up, the notion of building a young venture into a significant growth company was an opportunity that I just couldn't pass up. The fact that it was centered on teaching rock 'n' roll was right in my passion/purpose sweet spot. But five years later, in 2010, I was out of a job and my personal life was in free fall. This was now an obvious moment for me to lean in on security . . . or was it? While I was thinking about what to do and which professional path to go down, I chose to double down on trying to *optimize a plan* that took full advantage of *what I loved to do and what I was best at.* It simply came down to that philosophy.

As I was reflecting on my strengths, I also remember a nuanced conversation from earlier in my career. In 1991, I was ready to take on more responsibility and pitched a job that was going to be a significant step forward in my life. At that time, Barry Mayo, the president of the company, asked me a novel question: "What's your magic?" I was twenty-nine years old at the time and extremely driven to succeed, but I had never once really reflected on exactly what I thought I was best at. There is something counterintuitive about this. First, it is extremely hard to answer, and when I was asked that question, I responded with another question: "What do you mean?"

Barry laughed and said, "What do you think you do best? When you are firing on all cylinders, what exactly are you doing that brings you the most joy and the greatest results?" At that time, I remember quickly firing off a whole bunch of things: "I think I build great teams. I think I really understand people and coach well. I'm very creative and enjoy developing marketing strategies and solutions. I work hard, and I get stuff done. I like taking on big challenges. I'm not afraid to push people to perform. I focus on the numbers. I'm creative but also analytical. I can close big deals. I'm passionate about what I do, and I really want to help people grow and learn."

As I began spewing a whole lot of stuff, Barry started laughing some more. He could see the passion in me, and it turned into a really great conversation. He was hiring me for a position in Charlotte, North Carolina, and I would have to leave the comforts of New York City to help fix a broken business. This was going to be a massive growth opportunity on all levels. But it would also force me out of my comfort zone. I was a hardwired New Yorker moving to the Deep South, thrown into a difficult professional role that would require more sophistication and competence, and I was ready for the challenge.

While I was still developing my professional tool kit, I knew I was blessed with the tenacity to take on a lot of risk, both professionally and personally. This turned out to be a theme for me in my career. I took on the most difficult assignments: business turnarounds. Many years later, I learned that this challenge is slightly downwind from entrepreneurship. Building and rebuilding businesses are cut from a similar fabric; you must have a lot of confidence, the willingness to try things, the ability to move quickly, the capacity to get people aboard the train with you, the finesse to measure and pivot constantly, and so on. I was clearly entrepreneurial, but I never correlated it with the potential of starting my own business. Anyway, I got the job, and it turned out that Barry and his partner Lee Simonson became mentors for me at a pivotal time in my life.

Shortly after arriving in Charlotte, they asked me to participate in a series of personality profiles the Gallup® organization developed. That tool is now known as the CliftonStrengths® profile, and I have been using this system for the last thirty years to help me better understand myself and the people around me.[4] It allowed me to effectively coach others with their development, while also guiding me to maximize my own outcomes, whether they were professional or personal.

M = MAGIC. SO WHAT'S YOUR MAGIC?

In 2011, while trying to work my way through my professional reset, I sat in my basement with large pads all over the walls, trying to figure out what my career was going to look like. I found myself reflecting on my past in radio. I also thought about the fact that I got so much joy out of leading creative talent at School of Rock. I loved teaching creative types and professional musicians how to run a business. These folks were looking to learn and grow, and they were authentic and passionate about what we did. My self-analysis was confirmed via the results of my CliftonStrengths profile.

Here's how that works. After you complete their questionnaire, the profile ranks, in order, thirty-four different personality strengths from the ones that fire most often to the ones that fire least often. They group the strengths into four categories: Relationship Building, Executing, Strategic Thinking, and Influencing.

My number one strength is called *individualization*, and rather than get into a deep analysis, I can tell you it basically says that I am overwhelmingly interested in the unique differences in people. My second strength is *strategy*. I love to build things, build plans, create solutions, etc. (What a shock!) My third strength is *learner*. I can't get enough information and love to grow and think differently. My fourth strength is *positivity*. I count on myself to inject enthusiasm into the world. My fifth strength is *activator*. I like to move fast and get stuff done, with no BS. What Clifton told me perfectly aligned with what I knew to be true about myself. When I really thought more about my personality profile, other critical strengths also aligned with my capacity to build something.

Their profile is just a starting point if you are interested in understanding all the layers that influence your behavior. I have had hundreds of professionals participate in this, and every single one of them walked away with three thoughts:

1. Wow, that was really accurate.
2. I learned some cool things about myself that I wasn't very clear on.
3. It reinforces why I enjoy certain tasks a lot more than others.

As we shift back to the work you did when you created your **professional inventory**, your Clifton profile could help you to objectively clarify how you are wired and will inform the choices you make about your future.

We scored our professional inventory in chapter seven, and then we cast it against a series of questions.

How would you now respond to the following questions?

- Are you in the right company doing the right things?
- Is there an opportunity to grow and change within the firm?
- Do you need to look outside of your company to get what you're looking for?
- Perhaps it's bigger than that?
- Has the industry around you changed in a way that gives you less satisfaction or confidence that you can maximize your professional opportunities?
- Are there other things that you've always dreamed about doing?

Here are some more questions to consider:

- Is there a burning need to reset and redefine your professional path?
- Is there an opportunity to realign your role with the enhanced understanding of what you love to do and what you are best at?
- What's your *magic*?
- Is it being fully exploited so that you will be thrilled to continue your current career journey, or do you need to pivot now and build a plan to get to a new and more appropriate professional destination for the next phase of your career?

EVALUATE YOUR BODY OF WORK

As you reflect on your professional inventory and start to sort through a potential job or career shift, you must take the time to evaluate your body of work. It's one thing to say, "I'm a great accountant," or "I'm good at sales," or "I'm a great marketer," etc. However, it is another thing to truly understand your core personality traits as they relate to your natural tendencies and strengths. The range of possibilities is dynamic. You can make dramatic change happen or stay right where you are. Either way, you will reduce the stress in your life and enhance your health and happiness by investing in this work so that you don't miss this pivotal opportunity to align yourself for the future. Take some time. Remember, this process can be overwhelming, and if you find yourself frustrated or stuck, take a break and rejoin later.

To pull it all together, we are going to do a *personal evaluation* that will crystalize things at another level. Here's what I want you to do as the next step in our process.

1. Make a series of **observations (O)**, by writing in detail where you are in your job/career. What have you learned,

and what do you know to be true about your current and recent professional experience?

2. Under these statements, frame **your magic** (**M**) in a declarative sentence.

I want to share my personal evaluation from 2011 so that you can get a sense of what this looks and sounds like. Mine coalesced around the following thoughts:

- O: After twenty years in the media business and making a real career pivot into creative education as CEO of School of Rock, I was able to build the business into a one-of-a-kind brand, and this was deeply rewarding.
- **M: I am more prepared than ever before to start my own business, raise capital, and throw my heart and soul into building something that I am passionate about.**
- O: At age fifty, the grind of corporate America and the lack of control make it abundantly clear that I am willing to accept less money and need to be my own boss.
- **M: I will lean on my entrepreneurial sensibility.**
- O: Corporate politics and other nuances often get in the way of rewarding the most deserving performers.
- **M: Building and creating team culture is something I genuinely care about, and I want another chance to create a special place to come to work on my terms.**
- O: Things move too slowly in most companies, and I hate missing opportunities.
- **M: I like to move fast and really value getting things done without having to go through layers of bureaucracy. *The best ideas win!***
- O: I got so much joy out of leading creative talent at School of Rock. I loved teaching creative types and professional

musicians how to run a business. These folks were looking to learn and grow, and they were authentic and passionate about what we did.

- **M: I am extremely positive and creative. It is essential for me to be comfortable being myself while tapping into a kinder, more supportive, and deeply developmental leadership style that is focused on bringing out the best in creative talent and helping them maximize their potential.**

When you read my personal evaluation, you'll notice several things:

- It is abundantly clear that I was done working for others.
- For better or worse, I needed a new journey that would allow me to build something new from scratch.
- I wanted to be around art-centric/creative types.
- I had to lean in on my need to move fast and create a business culture where people would love to come to work.
- The fact that I had this question in my head—How come there are no cool art schools in my neighborhood?—was now *a problem that I had to solve,* and *I was going to do everything in my power to align myself with that challenge.*

YOUR FUTURE IS YOURS!

Changing your job or career path isn't for the faint of heart. For some, the process and the risks are just too great.

> So, do the work to adequately evaluate exactly how inspired and rewarded you are.

Life is about maximizing your health, happiness, and inspiration at the same time; it is hard when you don't know what you want or can't get what you want. So I implore you to go back to chapter seven and look at your professional inventory. If you scored less than 50 out of 60 in either one of the categories, there is an opportunity to take a closer look at your current state and perhaps close the gap without dramatic change. If you are below 40 for either section, you are scoring less than 66 percent, and in very basic terms, this is fair to poor. Given the fact that we are approaching the later stages of our careers and spend the bulk of our time at work, don't you deserve better than fair to poor?

For better or worse, I was unemployed in 2011, and my score was a mess as a result. However, I had huge opportunities for high-paying senior executive roles if I chose to pursue that. After doing the work to crystallize what would maximize my motivation, joy, challenge, autonomy, and control, I began germinating the idea for One River School. Once I started this, it opened a well of excitement for me. After months of evaluating the visual art space, I decided to become as much of an expert as I could in contemporary art in the shortest amount of time. This would allow me to build subject matter expertise to contextualize how to build an education concept in the space. So the work began and the *learner* in me was unleashed on the art world.

I signed up for six courses in NYU's continuing education program and earned a certificate in art business over eighteen months. I developed a business research project to understand the basic opportunity and needs in the marketplace, including a competitive analysis and all the other layers that would inform my business plan. I read countless books about contemporary art, traveled to art fairs, visited artist studios, explored galleries, and did all that I could to build my level of connoisseurship as quickly as possible. While I was never going to be a teacher of visual art, I needed to be able to taste the food and understand it well, and these skills would help me navigate the product development piece for our potential education concept. I was off to the races, and once my business plan was together, I raised seed capital to launch my venture and build proof of concept with the goal of *transforming art education®*.

In the process of launching and building One River School, I became connected to the idea that we were going to build something that didn't exist. I also knew how hard it was going to be and had the learning curve of School of Rock behind me. As Stephen Covey implies when he talks about proactivity, "If it is to be, it's up to me,"[5] and I loved the idea of taking on this massive challenge. In addition, I knew that I was going to grow in dynamic ways because of it. However, what I didn't know, which has become abundantly clear, is that I was blessed because this opportunity solidified the professional leg of my three-legged stool.

- Building an art education business allowed me to invest in others.
- My students and my team were going to be the beneficiaries of our business concept, and the quality of their lives would grow as a result.
- We were going to stimulate creative development in a generation of people.
- My interest in developing others was at the very root of it.

In the next chapter, we are going to focus on better understanding the role that *purpose* plays in our lives. It has become a compelling topic that we hear about all the time, and I believe that most of us don't really pay much attention to it. We have our families. We have our jobs. We have our bills. We have our friends. We have our persona that has been developed over approximately half of our lives. But, if you walk the path with me, you might find that there are some intriguing ways to look at your life differently as you think about the second half of it. And it may be the difference in maximizing your health and happiness.

Scan QR code for the downloadable or digital version of the assignment:

WHAT'S YOUR MAGIC?
Evaluate Your Body of Work

CHAPTER TEN

CLARIFYING PURPOSE

What Do You Really Stand For?

It has become so easy to flinch when you hear the word *purpose*. Sure, it's an overused term. Just browse the bookshelves and you cannot help but feel overwhelmed. However, a lot of what's out there misses the mark. The real question is, *Why should we spend our time thinking about what may feel like an esoteric topic that most have chosen to ignore?*

The concept of "finding your purpose" is an essential one, but if you don't have your personal and professional life in order, it is almost impossible to shift gears and allocate your time to this. That is why *Grow or Fold* requires you to focus on the first two legs of the stool to create the necessary stability to lean into the third critical component of your life journey. Keep in mind, all of this is not linear. Once you have goals and plans, you must do the work and continue to iterate over time. That is how we successfully navigate the future. And it helps if you welcome the bumps and the unpredictability in the road that you will encounter. There is never a perfectly straight line to your intended goal. To that end, growth, learning, and confidence are all the products of overcoming challenges.

So here is where we are at:

1. We began to do the work by taking our personal inventory.
2. We created a vision plan with goals and a commitment to change.
3. We clarified *our magic* and started to refine our professional outlook.

With that strategic work behind us, we are prepared to clarify our purpose. According to the *Oxford Dictionary*, the definition is

> "Purpose: the reason for which something is done or created or for which something exists."

Take a hard look at what you just read. As I sit here and write, I can't get over how compelling this definition is. Said differently, Your purpose is **your reason for living!**

If that is truly the case, how come so few of us:

- have been able to clarify this third leg of the stool?
- can communicate it succinctly?
- can crystallize it in writing?
- have committed our time to focus on it?
- have programmed it into our daily life?

I don't ask these questions to keep score. The truth is that we all had to live a good portion of our lives to learn and grow. To work and evolve. To make mistakes. Raise a family. Overcome hardships. Generate successes. And so much more. Then one day, we wake up and we are forty or forty-five or fifty or older, with tons of questions about where we are and where we are going. We often find ourselves struggling through complicated challenges, and we may be grinding through some of the most important life-planning experiences. Perhaps we also find ourselves thinking a lot about aging and our mortality for the first time.

Then, we all have that moment when we ask, *What the fuck is this all about?*

For me, it was organic. At fifty years old, and after thirty years in business and a tremendous amount of success, I was forced to reinvent myself for the third time. My health was now in question, and I faced intense challenges that left me feeling more vulnerable than ever. It was like I was playing defense rather than offense for the first time in my life, and I was scared about where I was going and needed to take control of my destiny. It wasn't simply a *midlife crisis*. It was bigger than that. Everything I stood for was in jeopardy. As I thought deeply about the magnitude of the issues I was facing, *I realized how short and precious my life was*. This led me to begin the journey I have been sharing with you, and it really started with the largest and most soul-searching questions I had ever asked myself:

- Could I reconstitute how I lived and learn to block out the noise?
- How would I manage the fear and anxiety of raising an autistic sixteen-year-old son who literally pulled the hair out of his head and was in the deepest and darkest teenage psychiatric breakdown you can imagine?
- How could I support and help my incredible wife, Susan, through the anguish, overwhelming sadness, and fear we had at home?

- Could we make sure Jason had a "normal" childhood while everything around him was abnormal?
- How do I manage my brothers, parents, and everyone around me who were looking to me to provide support?
- Could I manage the darker emotions, stress, anger, and real challenges I had that made life almost unbearable?

I felt deeply alone and not sure how I was going to rise to this challenge. So the bigger question became this: Could I step back and work through my challenges one day at a time, with a discrete sense of what the ultimate destination looked like?

That is what this book is all about. Life is about optimizing your experiences, day in and day out, so that you can achieve happiness, health, well-being, success, and more. But, at the highest level, it is about something more.

PURPOSE

This is also a concept that I personally had never spent any time thinking about. You may feel as if you are in the same boat. But, as I worked my tail off to reset things at fifty years old, a switch went off, and this concept went from a philosophical topic to *the thing* I had to figure out. The north star: the ultimate destination is a place where I could align my motivation with the goal to be the very best version of myself. This is what this became for me. It wasn't about money. It wasn't about success. It wasn't about anything external.

It was about a really simple question: **What do I really stand for?**

IN SEARCH OF THE COMMON DENOMINATORS

As we've worked together through the first eight chapters, I am sure it has become clear to you that a big part of my toolkit requires you to use your *own language* to frame important elements that help you map the essential direction of your life. It is one of the keys to building goals, strategies, and plans. This method allows you to build a *powerful emotional commitment* to create the energy and inspiration to put action into place. There are proven scientific benefits to committing to writing our thoughts, and we are going to dig in again and address what may be the most important thing of all.

To that end, think about how you would respond to the following statement:

> In my heart and soul, this is who I truly am.

This simple, thought-provoking concept is a powerful one. I am certain that it is a great place to start. As I worked through this assignment, I felt a sense of joy coming over me. The truth is, I have always been too concerned with what people thought about me. It is part of my genetic coding and has often led to frustration throughout my life. But, as I approached the goal of defining my purpose, it felt amazing to be as honest as I could be. This allowed me to be less inwardly focused and more accepting of who I am at the core.

Here is how I responded:

> I am an extremely positive person who is highly motivated to learn and grow, and I derive tremendous joy from helping others learn and grow. I love to solve problems and challenge myself to be the best I can be. I want to have fun and spend time with people whom I can learn from and who make me feel good. The more I can create joy for family, friends, and others, the happier I am.

Wow. This says a lot about me. In my own words, I have defined who I am in the world and not in terms of money, status, or labels. **It is about who I am and what I do for others**. And when I sanity-tested this against my personal and professional journey, it held true.

I continued to write and articulate more thoughts to frame:

> **Who I truly am**
> I want to make a difference—to give back and share what I have learned. I love to make people laugh and smile; I love to make people feel better; I love to help people think differently. I love to be liked by others who I am emotionally engaged with and spend time with people who have a passion for life. I have demonstrated this professionally by mentoring and investing in hundreds of people across my career who have worked directly for me. I build deep relationships with friends and family. I get great joy out of teaching people to be better professionally. I have worked very hard to be the very best I could be.

This exercise was cathartic! I wrote by speaking into a microphone which helped me more easily articulate a real and honest first-person perspective of myself. *Note:* For the first time in my life, I have publicly shared the most intimate, personal perspective to document and *own* my account of *who I truly am.*

Now the task is yours. Take ten minutes. Or an hour, a day, or a week. I want you to write down whatever pops out of your head to finish this statement: **In my heart and soul, this is who I truly am . . .**

- The key is to write and not be self-critical.
- Get as many thoughts as you can on paper and then start to edit it.

- Let it sit and come back to it to see what recurring themes bubble up.
- Pull out your phone and dictate into your phone if that works better.
- Once you have two or three paragraphs that succinctly tell a story about you and help define who you truly are, then let's move on to the next phase.

REFINE, EDIT, AND CRYSTALLIZE TO CLARIFY YOUR PURPOSE

I am now going to walk you through my method for refining your work. Below are the two paragraphs that I wrote and shared above. Within these paragraphs, I did the following things:

- I looked for themes to ultimately help me refine and crystalize my purpose into one succinct sentence.
- To do so, I searched to identify the most powerful themes that best align with the core of who I am.
- I then worked to sort the descriptions into three recurring groups.

NOTE: For the purpose of this book, I am going to use different "type treatments" to help demonstrate my process and to walk through my workflow. This will assist you in working through this important exercise on your own.

You will also find an engaging and helpful full color version of this exercise on my website by using the QR Code at the end of this chapter. The free resources at MattRoss.com will allow you to download your work and refine it at a relaxed pace, which can be essential to fine tuning your thoughts and creating clarity as you move towards a definitive understanding of Your Purpose.

IN MY HEART AND SOUL, THIS IS WHO I TRULY AM

I am an extremely positive person *who is highly motivated to learn and grow and* **I derive tremendous joy from** *helping others learn and grow.* <u>I love to solve problems and challenge myself to be the best I can be</u>. **I want to have fun** *and spend time with people I can learn from* **and who make me feel good. The more I can create joy for family, friends, and others, the happier I am.**

I want to make a difference—to give back and share what I have learned. **I love to make people laugh and smile; I love to make people feel better.** *I love to help people think differently.* **I love to be liked by others. I am emotionally engaged and spend time with people who have a passion for life. I build deep relationships with friends and family.** *I get my greatest joy out of teaching people to be better.* <u>I have worked very hard to be the best I could be</u>.

There were ***three themes*** that were consistent and dominant throughout my basic definition of who I am. I chose to take the actual descriptions and make a list for each cluster by grouping them by number and stacking them so I could better organize my thoughts. I also summarized the cluster with a simple description that helped structure the grouping.

Here's what it looked like:

1. **Positive, caring, and committed to spreading joy**
    - I am an extremely positive person.
    - The more I can create joy for family, friends, and others, the happier I am.
    - I love to make people laugh and smile; I love to make people feel better.
    - I love to be liked by others.
    - I am emotionally engaged with people who have a passion for life.

- I build deep relationships with friends and family.

2. Strategic and hardworking, committed to being the best I can be
   - I love to solve problems and challenge myself to be the best I can be.
   - I have worked very hard to be the very best I could be.

3. *Growth oriented and committed to helping others learn and grow*
   - Highly motivated to learn and grow.
   - Helping others to learn and grow.
   - Spend time with people whom I can learn from.
   - I want to make a difference . . . to give back and share what I have learned.
   - I love to help people think differently.
   - I get my greatest joy out of teaching people to be better.

Now I want you to look at the paragraphs you wrote that provide real insight into who you are. If properly expressed, these thoughts also tell some stories about what you are good at, love to do, and from where you derive pleasure and can be useful for helping others. Take your time to absorb your work, look for common themes, and use numbering to tag the common threads. Once completed, copy and paste into clusters like I did above and create one summarized description for each cluster. Take another look at my three clusters here:

1. **Positive, caring, and committed to making a difference and spreading joy.**
2. Strategic and hardworking, committed to being the best I can be.
3. *Growth oriented and committed to helping others learn and grow.*

WHAT DO YOU TRULY STAND FOR?

This exercise is hard, but it is essential to **clarify what matters most for the rest of our lives.** And if it is unreasonable, full of distortions, and unachievable, then it's important for us to refine our thoughts. Look at your three clusters and the most common groupings within them that describe what you stand for and who you are. Then, consider the following:

- Are they unattainable?
- Are they contrived, or are they rooted in thoughtful and sound logic?
- Are they aspirational labels, or are they universal ways of being?

We are not looking for something fancy or something grounded in an unachievable goal. We are looking for the very essence of your soul. In the fabric of your heart and mind, *what do you truly stand for?* After you have had ample time to do this work and can describe the key elements for each cluster, let's begin to true things up by taking your three summarized descriptions and putting them together in a way that gives you a first draft that will *start to form your purpose in writing.*

Here's what mine looked like:

> **My Purpose: First Draft**
> I am growth oriented and committed to helping others learn and grow. I am positive, caring, and committed to making a difference and spreading joy. I am strategic, hardworking, and committed to being the best I can be.

I had a weird sense of calm the first time I looked at this grouping above. I was proud that I was able to triangulate around this assignment and, in some profound way, really connect with not only who I was, but also what mattered most about who I would be in the future.

I read and reread this, and the more I did so, the more it aligned with something that I had never defined: *my reason for living.*

But something was missing. I'm not sure why but not seeing the word "creative" on the paper felt like an omission. The truth is, I was blessed with some real creative gifts, and at the age of forty-five, I began a professional journey of helping teach a generation of teens and kids to play music and tap into their creative sides. Now, I was building an art school and curating an art collection. I had spent a couple of decades managing creative people and felt adept at connecting with that side of my brain. I had written music, poetry, a blog, and a screenplay, but in the past, I never really felt that I could consider myself "a creative." I asked myself the following questions:

- Could I consider myself a creative entrepreneur?
- Where I deploy my creative sensibility and passion for helping others into my life's work?
- Could I continue to teach others around me to be more creative in developing strategies for business and life?
- Could I mentor and guide executives, and help my wife, sons, friends, and others grow and think differently?

This "other" motivator had to be part of my purpose!

So, I let things sit, and, after a few more days, I decided to simplify things but also mine for this other part of me that was essential to who I was. I stared at my first draft and reinterpreted it based on these additional thoughts. Here's what I wrote:

My Purpose

To do my best and share my positive spirit to lift people up and maximize our collective happiness by helping people live a

> more fulfilling and successful life, find their "magic," and tap into their creative spirit.

I loved it! But it was *too long.*

No problem. I have been taught in business to mine for simplicity. As I stared at these three lines, I decided I needed to reduce it to one or two lines. I needed to be able to say it succinctly. I decided I would copy and paste it and start to work on it by eliminating words.

Here is the next version:

> To do my best and share my positive spirit by helping people live a more fulfilling and successful life, "find their magic," and tap into their creative spirit.

Better, but still too long.

I copied this and edited it again with the goal of getting it down to no more than two lines that would describe my reason for existing. And this time I got it!

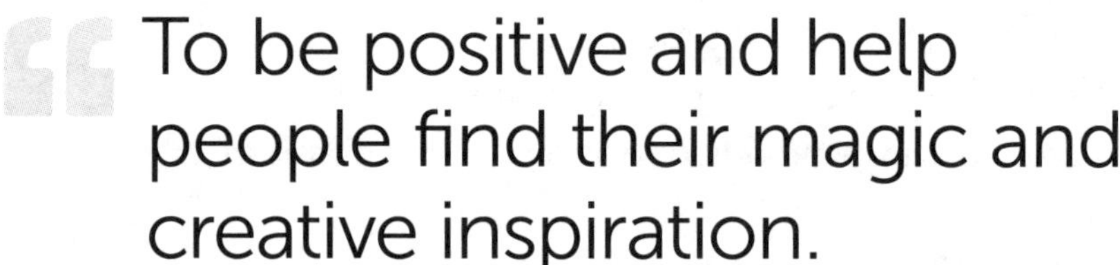

I was confused for a moment when I wrote this. It seemed so simple, but I was perplexed that I had never crystallized this before. There is no doubt that I get a tremendous amount of joy from helping others to grow, but I had always thought that it was my job to help people get better. *I never really thought that it was my reason for living*!

But the more I thought about it, this was obviously "me to the very core." And when you look at "my magic" via my CliftonStrengths, almost all my top strengths align around this: individualization, strategic, learner, positivity, developer, achiever, and arranger. This is my DNA and hard wiring.

My purpose crystalizes in a unique and personal way who I am, what I want to be, and what I will stand for over the duration of my life. So, let's review the process to make sure you wind up with a succinct and clear reflection of your purpose.

Here are the steps we utilized and a guide for you to chip away until you have clarified Your Purpose:

1. Write one to three paragraphs in your own words that define who you are in the world, not in terms of money, status, or labels. It is about who you are and what you do for others. Respond to this: "In my heart and soul, this is who I truly am."
2. Refine and crystallize your purpose. To do so, highlight recurring themes and identify the most common and powerful ones that align with your core. Identify clusters from the recurring themes to create groups.
3. Take the sentences and stack the similar ones by cluster so you can see the groupings and better organize your thoughts.
4. Label each cluster into a sentence to summarize exactly what the groupings communicate succinctly.
5. Create the first draft of your purpose by taking the sentences and stringing them together into one sentence.
6. Reduce it. Add a missing ingredient if that helps to define you.
7. Own it or refine it again.

PUTTING IT ALL TOGETHER: STAND ON THIS STOOL

I have so much profound respect for the work it takes to be happy. To tinker with who you are and what you want. To better understand your options and goals. To take control of the direction of your life and how best to use your time. It requires a major commitment and the ability to step back and evaluate who you are, what's working and not working, what skills and interests best define you, and what vision you have for yourself. So thank you for working through the last few chapters and working through some of the heavy lifting related to better understanding where you want to be, what you want to change, and how you need to behave to get there.

Note: This is not a race. It is a moment for you to cherish and work through at your own pace. How much you have done at this moment doesn't matter. What matters is how well you do this work when you are ready, willing, and able. Here are some pointers:

- Revisit the workflow at your own pace.
- Go to MattRoss.com for help.
- Use the QR codes in this book.
- Work with friends.

Take your time and be patient. It took me months to truly complete the three previous chapters, but when I did, it was clear that I knew what I wanted, had a solid plan to get there, and was highly motivated to get past the *dysfunctional safe zone*™.

So keep working at it. It may also be good to know that it is fluid and subject to change. The paint never really dries because you have the ability and power to erase and paint over your goals and plan at any point in time. This is a critical point. There is an ebb and flow to planning and execution that require you to constantly check where you are, and you are often called on to pivot to maximize your success. So don't worry about perfecting every element. Get comfortable with the primary changes that will drive you and go to work. You can then reflect and refine.

My journey is just one example. However, I have always believed that half the battle is getting started and moving in the right direction. Very simply, you build momentum one step at a time, and because I had a plan to tackle my personal challenges and a professional pathway that I was motivated to succeed at, it was very clear that I would be operating from a positive perspective, which was essential to who I was and how I needed to behave. After a couple of years, when I started to see things falling in line at One River School, I developed such pride in the fact that I was helping others, and it became abundantly clear that I had begun to put it all together and it wasn't a facade:

- I was chipping away at getting healthier and happier.
- I was discovering that I was born to help others grow and learn, and my professional ambitions were aligning perfectly.
- I was focused on figuring out how to simply be myself and not beat myself up when I wasn't my best.

And it all crystallized when I went through the process of clarifying my purpose. Here is the running dialogue in my head as I embraced my purpose:

1. **Be positive.**

   I will do everything I can to care for my family and friends and provide the support that they need. I won't worry when others aren't positive or when the world seemingly enjoys being angry. I will own the fact that I am a person who thinks the glass is 90 percent full most of the time and learn to love myself and my ability to lift others up.

2. **Help people find the magic.**

   I love to mentor, grow, and develop talent, and now that I am older and more experienced, I have more wisdom to share and need to spend my time doing this.

3. **Help people find their creative inspiration.**

   I am building One River School to *transform art education*®. We will deliver the most fun experience, which helps people create the most compelling artistic outcomes while also teaching them to think differently and to build their creative skill sets. That will allow them to have better problem-solving capabilities as they move through their lives, and it will help them truly appreciate their individual way of thinking.

Somehow, someway, I put it all together! It was as if lightning struck me. Not only did each leg of the stool provide massive support to the structure, but there was an integration that wove my purpose through my personal and professional life.

I was so lucky. Or was I?

Perhaps I just spent more time thinking through this than most other people. Maybe I was blessed with strategic talent that allowed me to step back and look at life thoughtfully. Maybe this process was a self-driven intervention that was going to transform my life in middle age. Or, had I worked so hard for so long but only now had the tools and motivation to Grow rather than Fold in the face of uncertainty?

I can't really explain it because it was organic. But somehow, I wound up with the clearest notion that I ever had about what would drive my happiness. **And my newfound purpose led to my goal of documenting my journey in this book!**

What better way to *be positive and to help people find their magic and their creative inspiration* than by telling my story and building a method that allows people to do the work on themselves?

We all live so transactionally, but this work is about strategically focusing on putting it all together. So let's look at the work you did before we move to the next chapter and switch gears.

Here is one last assignment that will ground you before we move on:

- Write down your three most important *personal goals.*
- Write down your three most important *professional goals.*
- Write down your *purpose.*

Is there a natural connection in these areas? As you move forward, think about what you can do to spend more time integrating your purpose into the essential personal and professional goals that you have established. How can you integrate your *reason for living* with clarity into your plan?

To maximize success across the three pillars, you need to summarize and be very clear about the work that goes into transforming your life into a different one. If you are still with me, it is because you are motivated to challenge yourself to behave differently, and the toolkit that we have been working through has allowed you to frame what is most important to you.

When I was working through this process, all the research that I read told me that *the difference between success and failure started with how specific I was about my vision for the future.* And from there, I could draw on the methods I have used in business to frame my goals, plans, and tactics. It's one thing to have a plan, and it's another thing to be able to function at a high level. Now it is time to go to work on ourselves so that we are enhancing our capacity to do great work.

Growth is a choice . . . Follow me.

Scan QR code for the downloadable or digital version of the assignment:

CLARIFY YOUR PURPOSE

PART III

THE POWER OF PURE GROWTH

There comes a time in every life—especially in the middle stretch—when strategy and reflection must give way to action and evolution. You've done the heavy lifting of looking inward, identifying what matters most, and crafting a road map to achieve your goals. But all that work is only the beginning. Now comes the true engine of transformation: growth.

Pure Growth isn't just about doing more—*it's about becoming more*. It's the deeply personal, often uncomfortable, and essential process of stretching who you are so you can reach who you're meant to be. And it becomes more critical—not less—as we age. Why?

Because time is no longer an abstract concept. We can feel its weight. We can feel its limits. And yet, we also begin to see how much potential still lies ahead—if we're willing to grow into it.

Part three of this book is where the journey turns from planning to expanding—from creating the blueprint to building the stronger, more vital version of yourself. It's about putting real fuel in the tank. And not just any fuel—this is about targeted, intentional growth in the three domains that most determine the quality of our lives: functional, emotional, and creative growth.

Each one feeds the others. Functional growth sharpens your tools—your memory, cognition, and problem-solving skills—so you can operate at a high level and fight back against the natural decline of aging. Emotional growth strengthens your resilience, interpersonal toolkit, and sense of internal calm. And creative growth reawakens your curiosity, opens new neural pathways, and helps you find joy and wonder again.

This isn't theoretical. It's deeply practical, and it's personal. I'll share how embracing this framework saved me—how it brought clarity in moments of grief, stability during uncertainty, and hope when fear was at its loudest. And I'll challenge you to engage with each area of growth in a way that fits your life, your goals, and your next chapter.

Let's be clear: You cannot coast your way through the second half of life and expect to thrive. You must grow each step of the way. You must push back against decay and distraction. And you must choose—every day—to become just a little stronger, a little more present, and a little more aligned with your highest self.

This is the work now. This is the path forward. This is the power of *pure growth.*

CHAPTER ELEVEN

THE POWER OF PURE GROWTH

I have an important mantra that has helped shape my adult life: *Plan your work AND work your plan*. This simple concept is one I have shared with everyone within the organizations that I have helped to build. I have also shared this with my family and friends because it gets at the heart of what I believe is required for driving success and happiness over time.

In the last four chapters, we spent a tremendous amount of time on planning because, without clarity and commitment to *what we want to achieve*, we are subject to living aimless and potentially meaningless lives. The process that we participated in was undoubtedly rigorous, but if you are serious about transforming your life and making substantial changes in middle age, it's necessary to think deeply about how you got to this point in your life and evaluate what was working and not working.

We then sorted through a vision for where you wanted to be and what you wanted to achieve in the future. After that, we created concrete goals and specific plans that provide a clear pathway for your personal and professional future. Lastly, we worked on articulating *your purpose* as a grounding influence on how you will behave to anchor your core sensibility of who you are and who you will remain. This was the icing on the cake, aligning the legs of your stool and helping to pull it all together.

Many factors influence your ability to successfully make all of this happen over time. This includes qualities like discipline, patience, hard work, ingenuity, self-awareness, stability, and more. But as we age, probably the most important component is rooted in one major element that we have yet to address: your commitment to *pure growth.*

> All the personal and professional planning in the world will not suffice on their own if you are not committed to getting better, smarter, and becoming more emotionally healthy over time.

The fact is, as we age, our bodies and our brains don't work as well as they once did. We lose muscle mass, and we lose brain matter. Our concentration declines. Our strength and stamina diminish. We struggle with change, and we are more subject to frustration and negative emotions. On their own, these changes present some of the most depressing things about aging that impact all of us. Genetics play a role, as does how we care for our physical health, but no matter who you are, how you are built, where you came from, and what you have done to date, *your commitment to personal growth and development is essential and the most profound antidote of all.* With all of this in mind, how many of us are really pushing hard against these forces and have laid out a defined plan to maximize our growth? Let's look at this concept a little bit more closely.

There are three separate areas of personal growth that each contribute to our overall capacity to thrive over the course of our lives:

- Functional growth
- Emotional growth
- Creative growth

Committing and investing in each of these will fuel the *pure growth* you need to maximize your capacity to accomplish your life plan. So let's begin to create a framework to fuel your journey. **I have devoted the next three chapters to these items,** but I want to share a snapshot of each now to whet your appetite and to give you a bit more perspective so that you can see the dynamic of **pure growth** laid out across three different areas of personal development.

- **Functional growth.** As you age, enhancing your functional development *improves your critical thinking* and allows you to tap into new tools that *enhance your problem-solving abilities,* while also working to *strengthen your memory and concentration.* Successful aging depends on your ability to acquire and master these tools as a driver of sustained success, health, and happiness.
- **Emotional growth.** As you age, enhancing your emotional development allows you to *adapt to change*, *build better relationships*, and *accept responsibility* for your behavior while seeking different and new perspectives that *fuel ongoing learning.*
- **Creative growth.** As you age, enhancing your creative development improves your brain's core *capacity to build new*

> *skills* which helps *generate new ways of thinking*. The capacity to adapt as we age is essential, and creative learning does this by producing changes deep within the structure of the brain that enhance brain fitness. And here is the added benefit: *Committing to creative learning supports your functional and emotional growth*—thus enhancing your quality of life and driving pure growth.

Each of these is one part of the pie, and you cannot fully develop or grow unless you cultivate and develop all three. Functional growth without emotional growth will improve your critical thinking but can prevent you from building strong relationships. Emotional growth without creative growth will help you to build relationships but you may remain incapable of adapting to environmental factors. Thus, we need them all to fully evolve.

MY MIDLIFE GROWTH JOURNEY

Let me take a step back and reconnect you to the moment in my midlife journey when I doubled down on my pure growth engine. After stepping away as CEO of School of Rock, I took a leap of faith at fifty to become a start-up entrepreneur. I had to learn new skills and dive into strategic planning, and after nearly two years of prep, I launched One River School in September 2012. I was all in—building the business, juggling two consulting gigs, and managing investments in three School of Rock franchises.

There was no guarantee of success, but I had a plan and was fully committed. During 2013, we were ironing out every kink in the model. I worked long hours on the ground as general manager, handling every customer interaction. It was exhausting—and exhilarating. For the first time, I had full professional control. No corporate noise. Just a clear mission to deliver an extraordinary experience for students, employees, and our community.

At the same time, something shifted inside me—something deeper, more personal. I felt alive. The past two years of taking classes, reading endlessly, visiting artist studios, attending art fairs, and immersing myself in contemporary art had expanded my mind. I was developing connoisseurship, building a collection, and feeling mentally sharper than ever. *That blend of functional and creative growth had a powerful impact.* My mood improved. My focus deepened. My ability to solve problems sharpened. One River wasn't just a professional venture—it became a lifeline that helped me navigate a storm of personal challenges.

That year, I watched my father's slow decline from Parkinson's. When he passed in September 2013, I felt a confusing sense of relief. For the first time, I understood what people meant when they said they were "glad" a loved one was no longer suffering. It marked a sobering reality: Midlife also brings some emotional terrain you can't control.

Meanwhile, Alex was on the mend and had entered a residential school in Maryland, almost five hours from home. Letting go was brutal. I felt guilt, sadness, and fear. Susan was torn up, and I wanted to protect her from unraveling. My mind spiraled with fears—rooted in old stories like Willowbrook, the infamous institution known for abuse. As you know, Alex is completely nonverbal, and whenever I would visit him, every goodbye left me in tears, wondering what he might have been thinking but couldn't say to me:

- Did he hate me for putting him there?
- Was he afraid?
- Was he lonely?
- Was he being mistreated?

These irrational fears consumed me. Add to that the chaos of my brothers, one of whom was now off the reservation and really struggling with suicidal ideation. The other was lost in mental illness and now living in subsidized housing that had safety issues tied to it. It was a daily and relentless wave of worry. Sleep became a chore. My mind wouldn't stop.

To survive it, I leaned into learning. I trusted my professional direction, but I knew I had to work on myself. I needed emotional growth: more patience, less impulsiveness, and better control of my intensity and worry. I needed to stay calm amid chaos and build a personal toolkit that could support me through my fifties and beyond. Despite my plans, it was clear—something deeper needed attention. I needed pure growth, urgently.

Amidst all of this, I harbored an obsessive thought that haunted me constantly: How do I avoid getting a neurodegenerative disease? After watching my dad decline from Parkinson's, I became consumed with preventing the same fate. I asked myself:

- Can I optimize how I think?
- Can I fight off something like Parkinson's or Alzheimer's?
- Is there a way to reduce the risk—or am I doomed by genetics?

I had to understand what was in my control. These questions launched a new phase of growth—one rooted in logic and science and aimed at managing both risk and worry. I brought all of this to my therapist. She specialized in families dealing with special needs and neurodegenerative diseases. That session was pivotal. She introduced me to *The End of Alzheimer's* by Dale Bredesen. For the first time, I had a road map—backed by research—that suggested prevention of neurodegenerative disease was possible.

That lit a fire. I read everything I could find, built a plan, and finally felt some control. My fear began to ease. I was creating structure—habits and strategies that supported both my physical and emotional health. It was a breakthrough. For the first time in my life, I was making real progress with my anxiety. And with that progress, I found myself thinking bigger: What else could I study, change, or build to fuel my pure growth?

That led me to ask these significant questions:

- How do I improve my ability to maximize my health? **Functional growth**
- How do I improve my quality of thinking so that I can take the energy that fueled my anxiety and worry and reposition it into positive thoughts about my future? **Emotional growth**
- How do I enhance my brain capacity so that I can live a long and happy life as opposed to one of premature aging and decline? **Functional, emotional, and creative growth**
- What can I do to manage my life, maximize my time, and enhance my overall personal and professional performance on a daily, weekly, and monthly basis? **Functional and creative growth**
- Can I create a new routine to maximize my happiness and joy? **Functional, emotional, and creative growth**

These questions led me to think more about *lifelong learning* and the pursuit of information to support my journey through midlife and into the future. I was certain that **pure growth** existed across these three areas, and the goal became to develop a comprehensive and disciplined approach to it. As I dug in to improve my capabilities, I found myself thinking like an educator who wanted to better understand the drivers of lifelong learning for myself so that I could share them with others.

LIFELONG LEARNING FOR US ALL

Think about this for a moment:

> To consistently behave differently, you must learn to think differently.

As a society, we spend so much time focusing on exercise and physical growth for the right reasons. But, at the same time, we spend such little time on *pure growth*, and I am not sure why that is the case. Perhaps our general life cycle has something to do with it.

The basic definition of lifelong learning is *the ongoing, voluntary, and self-motivated pursuit of learning for personal or professional reasons.*

That definition seems logical, but when do you think the term was first coined? According to my research, there is not a clear answer as to who came up with this concept, but the various attributions all center on the early twentieth century, somewhere in the 1920s and '30s. Wow! As a species we are one hundred thousand years old, but only in the last one hundred years did we address the definitive need to grow as we age. This makes no sense . . . or does it?

Let's look at this through the lens of evolution. Could you imagine people talking about AI or using an iPhone or streaming video 150 years ago? Of course not. Guess what, you also couldn't imagine their lives in any way, shape, or form. Think about this. As recent as 150 years ago, life expectancy in America was only about forty years. Very simply, the human species never had to worry about middle age and lifelong learning because their lives were short, and their quality of life was so difficult. But over the next fifty years, life expectancy grew by 50 percent and by 1925, people were living to about the age of sixty-five.

This trend continued to grow over the twentieth century, and people began to focus on the need to expand their horizons and adapt to their changing environment. As a result, the duration of life that we live today requires us to behave differently than our ancestors to enhance our brain's capacity, enjoy a long and rich life, stay connected with the speed of change in our society, and maximize our health and happiness. In addition, the speed and complexity of modern society also require more adaptive skills and modular thinking. Lastly, we need to grow to combat our aging body and mind and to ward off all the insidious external challenges that are often well beyond our control.

As you think about how you will proceed and drive your own *pure growth*, there are some other factors to think about. Self-limiting behaviors are common to almost all people, and I have discussed the concept of rationalization and *the dysfunctional safe zone*™. But other things get in the way of us learning new skills, reframing how we think, enhancing our sense of self, and rediscovering our passion for learning. And your personal traits may get in the way too. For instance, if your CliftonStrengths says that you are low in *learner*, you must be more vigilant than others to make sure that you are investing your time and effort to improve every day.

So it comes down to two simple thoughts:

- You must begin the process of creating change through a real commitment to learning.
- Everything you do today will govern how physically, mentally, and emotionally fit you will be for the balance of middle age and the duration of your life.

To that end, here are a few questions to consider:

- When was the last time you took a course?
- What three new skills are you working on to improve your performance and happiness?
- What creative hobbies do you have, and how much time do you spend on them weekly?
- Do you have specific behaviors that get in the way of your success or relationships?
- Are you working with a therapist or coach?
- Do you have access to the latest ideas that drive health and longevity?
- Do you have a concrete plan for personal improvement?

Answering these questions can provide some context to better understand what mental fuel you have been putting in your tank, what specific interests you have that may excite you to go deeper, and what habits need to be addressed for you to generate *pure growth.*

GETTING STARTED

When we launched One River School, I built a first-person view into the way adults thought about spending time on hobbies and their personal development, which was going to inform how I thought about education and driving my own growth. Ninety-five percent of our initial inquiries were focused on enrolling kids, and it was confusing to me, given the fact that all our advertising said that our programs were for "all ages and all levels." So I leaned in on what was becoming my purpose and made it my goal to enroll at least one hundred adults in year one to better understand how to create a world-class experience for adults.

After building and refining what we did, there were some *clear take-aways that I believe can help you in any active learning that you choose to do*:

1. **Try whatever excites you and aligns with the skill and creative development you need.**
   - There is some trial and error to this. The goal is to challenge yourself to tap into the childlike need to learn in all of us.
   - Split your time among functional, emotional, and creative learning so that there is a balance over time.

2. **Be a patient learner and be kind to yourself.**
   - Have fun. Don't be overly judgmental.
   - If you haven't been taking classes or reading self-help books for a long time, there is a muscle that comes with this.
   - If you haven't focused on your creative development in a while, get ready to feel a bit incompetent initially and

learn to love the challenge of stimulating your dormant creative capacity.

3. **Take in the room and enjoy the experience through your peers.**
    - If you are in a classroom environment, look around and take in your classmates.
    - Think about the commonality we all share and the joy of studying as a group.
    - Expanding your social network is vital, and these places are among the easiest to do so.

4. **The goal is not perfection.**
    - There is no scorecard except for the one in your head that sits in the center of *your ego*. Let it go!
    - The only thing you should focus on is attaining new ideas, new skills, new habits, new ways of thinking, and new friends.
    - How does that sound as a bevy of benefits?

5. **Take breaks and reset.**
    - Don't overdo it. I have periods where I will read five books in one month. Then I may not read anything new for two months. I have taken courses consistently for periods of time and then paused for other chunks of time.
    - The spirit of lifelong learning will become a habit, and once you get this in motion, you will figure out how much time and frequency to commit to formal learning and when to pause and restart.

Pure growth is a train that you want to be on.
Time to get on board.

CHAPTER TWELVE

FUNCTIONAL GROWTH

Sharpen Your Toolkit

Now that I've opened you up to investing in your *pure growth*, let's start with the most tangible aspect of this: **functional growth**. Think about it this way: Do you want to be smarter, healthier, and happier? You may think that is a silly question, but somewhere, someone answered no to all three of these just now.

Did you answer yes to all three?

Please say yes, yes, and yes ☺.

Okay, I don't mean to be so dramatic, but given everything that occurs in our lives as we age, most of us have become incredibly vulnerable to our own poor habits. Notwithstanding this trend, I have always been focused on *pure growth*. I may not have always been as consistent or clear about what areas I needed to prioritize, but I have always been obsessive about learning. Had this not been the case, I would have failed miserably in life because I didn't have much real mentoring, and I moved at such a quick pace that I often overlooked critical details.

Susan used to make fun of me because I have had my head deep into self-help books for my entire adult life. Very early in adulthood, I diagnosed that I was *deeply curious* AND at the same time, deeply anxious. So I became focused on building a functional toolkit that would allow me to Grow and not Fold. Over time, learning became a hardwired habit for me, but most of us struggle from a lack of investment made into understanding the best practices to drive our *functional growth.*

Remember the saying I shared earlier, What got you here won't get you there? We must grow and learn to think differently, or we will decline, and our skills will erode. Sound scary? It is. But investing in your mental capacity is at the center of what I'm talking about. How you push yourself to think differently is a function of the time you put in and the quality of the information you acquire. It also takes some real self-awareness and constant ego-checking because we all think we are smarter than we are. So let's dig into some key elements that will help you to function at a higher level and become more effective at achieving your evolving goals.

Let me share a simple story with you that demonstrates how we all can put our heads in the sand and run through obvious stop signs. I remember when I got out of college in the early 1980s and entered the workforce, there was a fabulous new trend that I saw happening all over Manhattan. The coolest bars and restaurants revolved around one thing: pasta! Yes, the world was mad over pasta, and it was easy to see why: It didn't cost a lot, it was easy to cook, the taste was amazing, and finally, it was "the best food for your health" (or so we were told).

Yes, the literature at the time and most health experts told us to stop eating all fats and consume carbs if we wanted to avoid heart disease and stay thin. I'm not sure about you, but for the next twenty-five years, 90 percent of my diet was carb based until I woke up one day with a metabolic disorder and was completely confused about how it happened. Then, at a moment's notice, carbs became the enemy, and "healthy fats" and a plant-based diet were thought to be what drove longevity, as demonstrated by the research of people living in *the blue zones.*

Here is the kicker. This information was available to me earlier, but I kept my head in the sand because I was addicted to carbs and loved eating bags of pretzels, drinking beer, shoveling pizza and pasta, and finding a way to fill my stomach with simple carbs that drove a sugar high. I ate like "Joe American," and I did so at the risk of my health and wellness. Now, let's get something straight:

- Am I going to tell you what to eat?
- Am I going to tell you how to exercise?
- Am I going to tell you how to live longer?

No! Why?

Despite the fact that I am all aboard the longevity train, I am not a leading expert in those areas, and countless resources are available to all of us to pursue that knowledge. Longevity research and enhancing "healthspan" are among the hottest topics today and new learnings are coming out every day. But if you triangulate your efforts around your *functional growth*, you will enhance how you think and build the tools that will help you avoid running through the stop signs that may impact your health and wellness.

YOUR TOOLKIT FOR YOUR FUTURE

Remember, *functional growth* is the practice of *enhancing your functional development* to improve your critical thinking. It allows you to tap into new tools that strengthen your problem-solving abilities, while also working to improve your memory and concentration. Successful aging depends on your ability to acquire and master these tools as a driver for sustaining success, health, and happiness.

So we are going to focus here on changing how you think so that you become an expert in recognizing when your metaphorical carbs are overwhelming the good stuff. This is what I mean by *sharpening your toolkit*, and

I often think that sustaining my ability to acquire new tools and make the right choices comes down to one of the simplest and most overlooked skills: the quality of the questions that I ask. On that note, here's a phrase that absolutely drives me crazy when I hear myself or others say it: "*My thing is . . .*"

All too often, I find myself sitting in a room, listening to a conversation among a group of people, and someone inevitably starts their reply to someone else's comment with this phrase. The truth is, it's become emblematic of how most of us behave in the modern era: We want to assert ourselves; we want to sound confident; and we want to share *what we know to be true*. The world has become so contentious, and we actually get rewarded socially online for hot takes and controversial opinions.

But the problem is, "we" are so programmed to react that *"we" often miss the critical opportunity to ask a simple question that might allow us to better understand the topic at hand*. This behavior is at the heart of one of the thinking styles that I have uncovered in my years of teaching leadership development. I define it as *declarative thinking*, and it comes with some benefits, but quite often it also drags along massive blind spots that impact personal growth and development.

So, if we are going to change how we think, we must change how we listen to others. That requires tremendous but attainable self-control. It also helps you better understand your thinking style, which we explore in the next section.

WHAT'S YOUR THINKING STYLE?

Change is hard, and changing how you think is at the root of ALL personal change and development. Your brain is wired to behave in a repetitive manner to create the fluidity and simplicity that are required to live your life and make thousands of decisions daily. But we must find a way to interrupt the patterns and habits that adversely impact our lives. So let's look at four clusters of thinking styles to better understand our natural response mechanism.

Below are four pairs of words that define a type of thinking style. Each of us has a behavioral style relative to how we process information and engage with the world depending on the unique combination of characteristics that make up your profile:

1. Inquisitive vs. Declarative
2. Patient vs. Impatient
3. Strategic vs. Tactical
4. Consistent vs. Variable

How would you define yourself? Look at the descriptions below for each, and after reading these, circle one word from each pair that most likely demonstrates your typical thinking style:

1. **Inquisitive vs. Declarative**
   - **Inquisitive thinking** is all about fostering curiosity and a desire to learn. It involves asking questions, exploring new ideas, and critically analyzing information.
   - **Declarative thinking** is a type of cognitive process focused on understanding and stating facts, concepts, or information clearly. It's about knowing *what* rather than *how* or *why.*

2. **Patient vs. Impatient**
   - **Patient thinking** is a cognitive approach that emphasizes taking the time to reflect, consider options, and carefully evaluate situations before acting.
   - **Impatient thinking** refers to a cognitive style characterized by a desire for quick answers, immediate results, and rapid decision-making.

3. **Strategic vs. Tactical**
   - **Strategic thinking** is a forward-looking cognitive process that involves planning, anticipates future scenarios, and makes decisions aligned with long-term goals.

- **Tactical thinking** is focused on the short-term execution of plans and actions to achieve specific objectives.

4. **Consistent vs. Variable**
   - **Consistent thinking** refers to a stable and coherent approach to processing information and making decisions.
   - **Variable thinking** refers to a flexible and adaptable approach to problem-solving and decision-making.

When I created this exercise, I was able to reflect on some natural tendencies that were helping me grow, but it also shed light on tendencies that were often getting in the way of my growth. To be clear, we all possess some of each of these, but when you make your choice for each, you need to select the one word for each pair that most often reflects your thinking style.

Matt Ross thinking style:

1. Inquisitive
2. Impatient
3. Strategic
4. Variable

This is the combination that most often defines my thinking style. Without a doubt, my creative brain leans in on thinking broadly and challenging the boundaries of what is possible. Having said that, I am also cursed because I am deeply impatient. But, in some weird way, the two work together because if I didn't have impatience, I would spend all my time thinking! Thankfully, my intense urge to get stuff done fast drives my ability to execute and is a strength that my CliftonStrengths profile reinforced. (*Activator* is one of my top strengths.)

I often tell people who work for me that "my goal is almost always to get to the best solution, one that provides me with at least a 95 percent confidence rate, as fast as possible." And it just so happens that this trait is one that aligned me with entrepreneurship and has driven success for me in business and generally in life. However, my impatience has also caused impulsivity and false confidence in my solutions.

So one of the key components within my *functional growth plan* has been focusing on slowing down and not being so quick to determine a solution. I have learned to ask more questions and probe deeper into what others were thinking so I could better understand other points of view. This has also helped me to build *emotional growth* because I've learned that through patience, I could develop more tolerance and acceptance of others, rather than being thin skinned and taking things personally. I remain a work in progress, and I am constantly searching for ways to challenge my need for speed, while also developing tools to help me stay on course and execute consistently. Getting from point A to point B requires lots of discipline, and I continue to work at this by committing to ongoing education, self-evaluation, and feedback from others.

So, what was your thinking style?

- How would you identify your natural tendencies to make decisions and to respond to incoming information?
- Are you somebody who puts their head in the sand and stays focused on getting stuff done, or are you somebody who is open to new ways of getting things done?
- Do you move too fast or not fast enough?
- Do you ask probing questions or love to focus on the facts at hand?

Keep this in mind: I'm not here to be judgmental about anything. However, if your tendency is to be deeply tactical, you better have great confidence in your plan because you may be missing new ways to improve or enhance how you make decisions. The checklist is important because it also enables you to look at your CliftonStrengths, your body of work across your lifetime, and more importantly, the last five to ten years, both professionally and personally. Look at what is really bugging you, and ask yourself the following questions with honesty and curiosity:

- What are you struggling with?
- What tendencies get in the way of improving and enhancing your outcomes?
- How solid are your core relationships?
- Do you have the capacity to break bad habits?

From here, you can establish a plan to improve your functional skills, which will enhance your critical thinking and ensure that your problem-solving capabilities get better as you age. Along the way, you just might also become better at how you relate to others and think about your future growth and potential to achieve your goals.

THE POWER OF QUESTIONS

Here is my favorite question: *Can you tell me more?* In fact, these three words, "tell me more," are powerful, and I will share with you how to use this simple tool to improve your ability to drive *functional growth.*

Early on in my sales career, I was blessed to have an incredible training resource who helped me best understand how to be effective. The key to building great customer engagement was *to understand the customer's needs from the customer's point of view*, which meant I needed to be prepared to ask as many thoughtful questions as possible to *really understand what they were trying to achieve in their words*. In fact, I was taught to "avoid selling them something" until I could share back exactly what their goals were verbatim. You see, they knew their business better than I did, but they were looking for me to create problem-solving marketing solutions that would drive revenue growth. Inevitably, I always found the most powerful thing I could say was "tell me more." It would often lead to a flurry or two that was hiding just below the surface, which provided the nuance and context to understand exactly what their most pressing needs were.

Improving the quality of the questions we ask can lead to deeper insights, more effective problem-solving, and better communication. And in many ways, the challenge of driving your functional growth comes down to the quality of questions that you are asking yourself and the questions that you ask of the people around you.

Here are five ways to improve the quality of your questions:

1. **Be specific.**
   - Provide enough background information for the person to understand the context of the question.
   - Example: Instead of asking, "Can you explain this?" ask, "Can you explain how this solution addresses the specific challenge we discussed?"

2. **Check your biases.**
   - This helps avoid leading questions and promotes a more objective dialogue.
   - Example: Instead of asking, "Why don't you support this idea?" ask, "What are your thoughts on this idea?"

3. **Use follow-up questions.**
   - Don't settle for surface-level answers. Use follow-up questions to probe for more detail or clarification.
   - Example: If someone says, "It was difficult," you can ask, "Can you explain what made it difficult?"

4. **Be open to multiple answers.**
   - Don't ask questions that suggest the answer you want to hear. Instead, phrase them to allow for multiple perspectives.

- Example: Instead of asking, "Don't you think this approach is the best?" ask, "What are some pros and cons of this approach compared to others?"

5. **Consider timing and tone.**
   - Asking a good question at the right moment can make a huge difference. Ensure the tone of your question is respectful and curious, rather than confrontational or dismissive.
   - Example: "You always have a thoughtful perspective, how do you feel about . . . "

And for bonus points, probably the most important piece of all is **practice active listening.**

By *listening carefully,* you can craft more informed follow-up questions, which drives a deeper and more engaging connection, allowing for better understanding of the subject matter.

LET'S REVIEW

Understanding some of your most basic natural tendencies can be at the root of driving your functional development. By better understanding **your thinking style,** you will enhance your ability to overcome the natural tendencies that get in the way of acquiring critical information. And whether you are dealing with personal or professional challenges, your advocacy in these areas is what leads to the outcomes you seek. If you work to *improve the quality of the questions you ask*, you will develop a new habit that generates more insight and thoughtful engagement all day and every day. *How actively you listen to others* is perhaps the most underrated component of all, and your investment in better understanding all these drivers will help you maximize your engagement with others, and, most importantly, improve the quality of the decisions you make that govern your future.

The goal of this chapter wasn't to tell you what subject matter you need to work on. It was to provide some new functional skills that would enhance your core competencies and help you to develop your functional growth plan. The process of learning and gaining insights to generate growth involves the ability to think, reason, and organize thoughts and ideas to better understand the world. Functional development in middle age involves the ongoing growth and maintenance of various physical, cognitive, and psychosocial abilities, and here is the key piece: Your success is dependent on your ability to advocate for yourself, which starts with figuring out the most critical areas that you need to focus on. Here are some examples of domains to focus on as you build your functional growth plan:

- **Physical improvements.** Regular physical activity, especially strength training, cardiovascular exercise, and flexibility practices (such as yoga), can help maintain physical and cognitive functioning.
- **Lifelong learning.** Engaging in new learning opportunities, whether through formal education or hobbies, can support cognitive health and improve memory and problem-solving abilities.
- **Healthy diet and lifestyle.** A balanced diet rich in nutrients, adequate sleep, and stress management techniques contribute to overall well-being.
- **Social connections.** Maintaining strong social networks and relationships promotes mental and emotional health, reducing feelings of isolation or depression.
- **Purpose and meaning.** Volunteering, mentoring, or pursuing passions can foster a sense of purpose, contributing to positive psychosocial development.

Functional growth isn't about reinventing who you are—it's about refining how you think, how you act, and how you show up in every area of your life. In this chapter, we've explored the critical importance of identifying your natural thinking styles, the value of high quality questions, and the powerful roles that curiosity and self-awareness play in shaping your ongoing development. These are not abstract theories. They are tools—practical, actionable tools—you can start using immediately.

If there's one central takeaway, it's this: Growth is not automatic. It's intentional. And your ability to adapt, improve, and evolve hinges on your willingness to challenge your current assumptions and interrupt your habitual patterns. Whether it's asking, "Can you tell me more?" or pausing to reflect instead of reacting, these small shifts compound into lasting transformation.

So now it's your turn. It's time to assess your patterns. Refine your instincts. Ask better questions. Listen more actively. Sharpen your toolkit with the same intensity and purpose that you'd apply to anything you truly want to master.

Because the truth is, you already have what it takes to grow. Now, you just need to apply it with intention. Your future—your health, your happiness, your effectiveness—depends on it.

Scan QR code for the downloadable or digital version of the assignment:

FUNCTIONAL GROWTH
Sharpen Your Toolkit

CHAPTER THIRTEEN

EMOTIONAL GROWTH

Optimize Your State of Mind

Are you ready to do a little soul searching? The root of emotional growth is understanding yourself and identifying the behaviors that hold you back. Emotional growth is something I am keenly interested in because life has taught me that it is very hard to optimize our state of mind and stay out of our own way.

I'm a perfect example of someone who has struggled in this area. I was blessed with lots of skills and a robust personality driven by my passion for life and fueled by a wide range of emotions. My energy and fierce determination to succeed have been a strength, but my impulsiveness, anxiety, repetitive thinking, and penchant for taking things personally required constant self-management and often created tremendous stress. In general, life is so damn hard, and it is even harder when we don't work to understand the factors that influence how we think. To that end, let's dig in and take a closer look at this concept.

As you age, *enhancing your emotional development* allows you to *identify and regulate your emotions, organize your thinking,* and *optimize your thought patterns.* You will also get better at adapting to change, building relationships, accepting responsibility for your behavior, and seeking out different and new perspectives that fuel ongoing growth. That is, in essence, the definition of emotional growth.

It is at the base of the pyramid that drives our performance because *the complex challenge of regulating our emotions impacts all that we do in addition to influencing our functional growth.* Take these examples:

- If we constantly run hot and are always on edge, chances are we will not be able to process information patiently and respond properly.
- It's also likely that it'll be harder to stay on task.
- We may even find ourselves overwhelmed and confused about what our priorities are.
- What if you are angry or depressed?
- Or worrying and anxious nonstop?

There is a litany of emotions that can impact our behavior and ultimately, our success. However, we have also learned that our growth and happiness are directly tied to how effective we are at managing stress and ultimately, regulating our emotions. The science has become crystal clear over the last few decades—our brain is a soup of chemicals that rise and fall based upon a few factors. Certainly, our DNA, personality, and natural wiring are significant parts of this, but the chemicals that we produce—including adrenaline, cortisol, dopamine, and serotonin—have a dramatic impact on our behavior.

How we manage our stress also influences how we maximize our sleep, which may be the single greatest contributor to balancing brain chemistry. So what are you doing to optimize your state of mind and drive your emotional growth so that you can take control of your health, happiness, and productivity?

FINDING EMOTIONAL BALANCE

When you drive a car fast, the motor is going to get hot. The same is true when you pursue ambitious goals or face significant life challenges. Your brain, an engine in many regards, is going to need enhanced systems to manage it. There are no two ways about it; the complexity and speed of life are different today, but our reptilian brain, which was created one hundred thousand years ago, is still trying to adapt to modern living. Think about how many inputs we are confronted with every day. One piece of research suggests that we make on average thirty-five thousand decisions a day!

On some level, it is amazing how efficiently and effectively our brains work given the volume that we throw at it. But, when you start to add acute challenges, life planning, constant societal noise, and the effects of aging, learning how to best process things becomes a complicated art form. Your brain is always at war. The information you're being bombarded with is the equivalent of incoming missiles, so *how you filter information is the key to maintaining your emotional balance.* And maintaining emotional balance is a core requirement for generating emotional growth and functional growth.

For example, here's a scenario that we all face every day:

> We wake up, turn on the news, and see that there's a terrorist act or some other crisis. BAM! That's the equivalent of a targeted missile for your adrenal system. You drive to work, and someone cuts you off. BAM! That's another missile. You are at lunch, and somebody brings up politics, or somebody confronts you about something that they think you did wrong. BAM!

These are all missiles, and somehow, someway, we must find a mechanism for sorting out the components in life that are essential to focus on. So let's get to work and start to utilize the most simple and effective tool possible for maintaining emotional balance.

> Every time I am faced with something that concerns me, I quickly think about the relative amount of control I have on influencing it.

Don't get me wrong, I am passionate and care about many things in society on an intellectual basis, but for me to be stable, balanced, thoughtful, and in control of my emotions and performance, I can't chase every challenge and regularly debate them, because I tend to get completely and emotionally engaged when I do. So I save the complete emotional engagement for the things that I can influence—my time, how I treat my friends and family, how I take care of my health and wellness, how I matriculate on my plans and goals on a personal and professional basis, how I manage my financial affairs, and how I stay dialed in to living my life through my purpose.

This is a relatively new discipline to me; it is something that I mastered in midlife as a result of the daily work I have been doing. When I was younger, no matter how hard I tried, I sucked at it. As a result, I drank too much alcohol, never slept well, worried nonstop, and tried to thrive on the adrenaline of life while battling all the emotional swings that came from it. But I have demonstrated tremendous emotional growth over the last decade. I built new tools to achieve my goals, and for the first time, I feel in complete control of how I behave and the decisions I make. And I could not be prouder of myself because I chose to prioritize my emotional growth and found a way to allocate the necessary time, money, and effort that was required to accelerate this growth.

One of the most important resources that I credit for driving my personal growth is the teachings of Stephen Covey and his seminal book

The 7 Habits of Highly Effective People. Over the years, I have given this book to many people, and there is always a copy nearby for me to refresh on critical elements.

The topic of **circle of control vs. circle of concern**[6] is among the most powerful and elegant methods for me to avoid "chasing negative thoughts." Let's work on an assignment that will walk you through how this works:

1. **Make a list of the things that concern you today.**
    - The list can be super comprehensive, or, for today's purpose, it can be an abridged version of all the things that concern you in your life.

2. **Draw a large circle around everything that you just wrote.**
    - This is your *circle of concern.*

3. **Now, circle each specific item on that list that you have control over.**
    - This means you have direct, personal influence on the potential outcome, and it is not theoretical.
    - Think of it this way: You can contribute real time to solving these problems on a daily, weekly, and monthly basis, and it is proven that your behavior is required to influence the outcome.

4. **Everything that you just circled makes up your *circle of influence.***

This is where it gets tricky. Why? Because we are dealing with our emotions here, and they often drive us to chase the things that speak to our values and our sense of what is right or wrong. For example, you may have a strong emotional connection to the climate crisis, inflation, politics, or our infrastructure. I get it. These concern me too. But I want us to focus on how we regulate our emotions when we discuss these things.

My list of concerns is unbelievably long, but when I look at how I spend my time and where I am contributing real effort to solving problems, that list is not as long, and it is precious. My son Alex is one of my greatest concerns in life. And while there is a fair amount that I must rely on others for his care and safety, how I advocate for my autistic adult son is near the top of my list of things that I am focused on influencing.

> "It comes down to mastering the art of emotional filtering, and this precious, learned, and manageable behavior is often the difference between people who regulate their emotions and those who don't.

If you're making thirty-five thousand decisions a day and you're letting your mind wander and argue and debate and worry about countless things that you have no control over, chances are, the quality of your decisions will decline. *The 1 percent of your daily decisions that are mission critical to your life is where you must excel!* As we just reviewed in the previous chapter, our thinking style, listening ability, and habits often dictate how we process information. And these skills have become embedded over our lifetime, so when you get to middle age, it is extremely difficult to change who you have become. But that's why we are here and talking about growth, people!

If you want the best outcome for the second half of your life, don't stay in the *dysfunctional safe zone*™ and make the same mistakes for the rest of your life.

Think about who you are, who you want to be, the things you want to achieve, and the emotional growth required to drive your health, happiness, and success! *This should be in your circle of concern and influence* because you can change how you respond to the environment at large with practice.

Let's keep going.

DON'T CHASE THINGS—PUT THEM ON THE SHELF

I owe a lot of my emotional growth over the last decade to the work I have been doing with a top-tier therapist. Ilana Rosenberg is smart, logical, practical, and caring and has a lot of thoughtful tools that have improved my ability to optimize my thinking. Our sessions have helped me work on the challenges that I have faced, while also building tools to enhance my emotional growth. And the work I have done has guided me through some of the overwhelming complexities that I faced in midlife.

I remember one day early on in a session when she asked me if I had heard of the concept of *cognitive distortions*. In essence, we are all prone to distorting reality based on how we interpret the information at hand. Some of us have the natural tendency to blame others for our outcomes. Others tend to catastrophize things and blow them out of proportion. Sometimes we may jump to mind reading or personalize things. It is so hard in real time to not fall prey to one of the many different potential cognitive distortions. *The key is to recognize when distortions have crept into your processing of information so that you can manage your potentially adverse responses.* And this tool has helped me keep my balance time and time again since I began to deploy it.

All right, I'm going to go down this rabbit hole a little bit further to share another example that may shed light on a typical emotional challenge that we face.

One of my common distortions is I tend to personalize things. Not sure if this is my DNA or a function of the environment that I grew up in as the youngest of three boys, but there is no question that somewhere deep in my gut is a sensitivity that on the one hand, drives me crazy, but on the other hand, has helped me successfully connect with people. There have been so many times in my life where I have quietly stewed on or overreacted to something that someone said or did when I could have simply done a better job at managing my emotions. In my twenties and thirties, I was probably not ready to deal with this head-on. But somewhere in my mid-forties and early fifties, as part of my commitment to emotional growth, I took a good look at myself and realized that all too often I acted like a big fucking baby!

As I write these words right now, I feel like erasing them, but I'm going to own them and leave them here for eternity.

The truth is, I could remember losing my mind when I was picked on as a kid. I couldn't stand it then, and I can't stand it now. When I started to really dig in and do this work, I realized that my acute sensitivity created a distortion force field around people's true intent. And when I went deeper, I realized that all too often, my interpretation of others' intent was wrong.

For example, when someone made a joke directed at me, maybe they weren't making fun of me with any malice. Or perhaps when someone rolled their eyes, they weren't questioning my intelligence. Perhaps when I wasn't greeted with the warmth that I hoped for, maybe I was just personalizing it and distorting reality. Don't get me wrong. I'm not on edge all the time; I'm not Larry David. But I did become aware that I needed to work on not taking things personally so that I wouldn't inappropriately escalate conflict in my head that didn't exist.

Another emotional challenge for me was my tendency to ruminate. Just like my sensitivity, this trait was quite often a strength in my career because I developed an unrivaled level of persistence that wouldn't rest until I achieved my intended goals. I also built great strategy by obsessing over my options, resources, and plans. However, it also worked against me by fueling my anxiety and worry about things that were harmful to my emotional state. For example, if I felt a strange pain or went to the doctor and had an abnormal test result, I would immediately project the worst-case scenario, and I wouldn't be able to shut it off. This would lead to projecting the worst possible outcomes and sleepless nights.

And the internet didn't help. As we got older and had access to big information, I would research every aspect I could find, even to the point where I was reading studies from the National Institutes of Health that were truly meant only for doctors and professionals in the space. There I was, deciphering medical research and looking at tables of data to better understand whether I was at risk to ultimately get the worst-case scenario. And the deeper I dug the hole, the more stressed out and worried I became. You wouldn't know it if you met me, but given all the personal crises I was dealing with in midlife, I was very vulnerable to cognitive distortions. I had so many things circling through my brain that I was constantly super stressed, and this way of living was simply not sustainable. Building my emotional growth plan became an essential goal for me to transform myself in midlife.

Then I had a real aha moment.

One day, when I was sitting at home, something popped into my head that scared the shit out of me. I felt the stress and adrenaline quickly building in my chest, but something happened this time that turned out to be a pivotal moment for me. I don't know why, but I paused, looked across the room, and began staring at my bookshelf. And as my eyes started to scan the books, I began to think of each of the books I was staring at as representing a scary or negative thought. I proceeded to tell myself that *maybe I don't need to pull a book out right now* and *maybe I can fight the urge to chase the negative thought*. Perhaps I could *leave it on the shelf*, or, if I started to *pull the book out* and dig into something that would take me down a negative rabbit hole, maybe I could just empower myself to *put the book back* or *take the book out later* if I wanted to do so. It was that simple.

A switch went off. I had developed a behavioral intervention that was purely mine; it was one that allowed me to press pause on negative thoughts before they escalated into worry and repetitive thinking. Perhaps I could summon the same technique in the future to interrupt my tendency to quickly grab onto something, distort it, internalize it, and shift my emotions. So, for the next few weeks, whenever something appeared that pissed me off, frustrated me, or scared me, I would pause and say out loud, "Don't chase it." Then I would pause and say, "Put it on the shelf." From there, I started to take the most difficult and emotional topics, and I would visualize taking a book and putting it back onto a bookshelf.

To reinforce this, I would summon that physical feeling you get once you've closed the cover of a book and stuck it back on the shelf. This sequence turned out to be such a beautiful metaphor, and because there was a visual and physical component to it that I could lean on, it seemed to produce a more bankable and successful way for me to stop the flow of negative energy tied to distorting new information and prevent me from beginning the adverse loop that comes with it.

Each time I caught myself and deployed this new habit, I generated positive emotions and positive brain chemicals that allowed me to feel in control, happier, and more confident!

I would pat myself on the back and literally say, "Great job not chasing that bullshit." Wow! I now had a new go-to and simple way to avoid the repetitive loop that came with my adverse response to information. I now had control over the incoming missiles, and I could at my own choosing go back and "grab a book" to revisit any emotional topic on my terms. When I shared this learning with Ilana, I remember her reflecting on the breakthrough I had made. It was such a great feeling to also appreciate and reinforce the work I was doing because, if I were to change, I had to apply her teaching when she wasn't in the room.

After talking about the sequence and the experiences I had, Ilana shared a book that would continue to create context for the work I was doing. The book, *Man's Search for Meaning*, was written by Viktor Frankl, and it tells the compelling story of a Holocaust survivor in his own words and the challenge of managing his emotions as he suffered through one of the most inhumane moments in our history. Ilana specifically focused on an amazing quote[7] from the book that instantly stuck with me forever:

> "Between stimulus and response lies a space. In that space lies our freedom and power to choose a response. In our response lies our growth and our happiness.

I think of this quote constantly when I am frustrated by an emotional missile. The space that I learned to create for myself was the required first step for me. And it was powerful because I also realized that I wasn't just distorting things because I was sensitive, I was also responding too quickly to everything. *I needed to just let that space between stimulus and response occur more frequently and for a longer duration.*

If you think about pausing before you react, asking better questions, and probing your personal sensitivities and your tendency to produce cognitive distortions, **you will be setting yourself up for emotional growth.**

And the more you do it, the more it will work. Along the way, you will:

- be calmer,
- become a better listener,
- not be so reactive,
- grow to be more thoughtful, and
- be a better contributor.

And you may not need:

- attention,
- to control things,
- to be right, and
- to be the center of attention.

These are the curses that plague many of us—which of these describe your emotional challenges that need to be addressed?

By focusing on understanding the cognitive distortions that get in the way and create challenges with people in your life, you will drive emotional growth that will fuel better performance, enhanced mood, improved relationships, and a new sense of self. By the time we get to midlife, our existing personality traits are deeply ingrained, but once you get these in check and take greater control over how you direct your thoughts, you will improve every aspect of how you feel about others and the world at large.

On my website, **I share more about cognitive distortions** with material that will allow you to work on better understanding yours. It is one of the best exercises you can go through because the first step is to understand your personal tendency to distort the information around you. Understanding the distortions that got in my way was one thing, but interrupting those sequences to avoid getting angry, frustrated, or worried, or projecting some horrible outcome, was the work I needed to do.

THE SEARCH WITHIN

It is one thing to tell yourself that you need to improve your diet, exercise more, or make a career shift. These are the kinds of changes that most of us focus on. But changing the fabric of *how we think*, *how we respond to others*, and *how we process information* remain some of the hardest changes to make.

We have our natural wiring to overcome and a lifetime of encoded habits that influence our automatic behavior. I have shared a lot of personal stories that reflect the specific aspects of my personality that I knew got in the way of my ability to be the best person I could be. There was no sense for me to stay in the *dysfunctional safe zone*™ if I could change. The key is that I was motivated to grow.

So, let's spend a few minutes right now to **think about the recurring behaviors that adversely affect your happiness and create other emotional challenges.**

1. What are the three to five things that you wish you could change about yourself and how you relate to others?
2. What are the three to five things that get in the way of you feeling pure joy?
3. What are the three to five things that others might say about you when they are talking about your worst possible traits?
4. When you feel angry or anxious, how do you typically behave?

Before you can build a plan to grow, you must be willing to open yourself up to the most frequently recurring and self-limiting behaviors that have become hardwired habits affecting your emotional state and limiting your capacity to grow emotionally.

Are you willing to do this? Or, said in a different way, are you willing to not do this?

GROW OR FOLD?

This is your license to be self-critical in the purist sense possible, and you will be shocked to see how incredible it feels to truly understand the thought processes that get in the way of your health, happiness, success, and ability to grow over time.

Scan QR code for the downloadable or digital version of the assignment:

EMOTIONAL GROWTH
Optimize Your State of Mind

CHAPTER FOURTEEN

CREATIVE GROWTH

The X Factor

You had to know that this was coming. Given my twenty years in the creative education space, my passion and profession aligned in a way that has already changed the life of countless people, including myself. Remember my purpose? *To* ***be positive*** *and to help people* ***find their magic*** *and* ***their creative inspiration.*** Therefore, I wouldn't be demonstrating my commitment to fulfilling my purpose if I didn't get deeply into this topic to assist you in this process. So let's look at what goes into *lifelong creative learning.*

What if the secret to a sharper mind, a stronger emotional core, and a more joyful existence is already inside you—just waiting to be unlocked? For decades, we've been sold the idea that creativity is a luxury, a talent reserved for artists, musicians, or "the gifted." But what if I told you that creativity is not just for hobbies—it's a lifeline? A tool for navigating life's most complex challenges, managing stress, building resilience, and growing into the fullest version of yourself.

This chapter is a wake-up call. A personal and practical invitation to reignite your creative engine—because creativity isn't just an outlet for expression, it's the X factor for transformation. I've spent over twenty years witnessing thousands of people—kids, teens, adults, professionals, parents, retirees, beginners, and experts—radically reshape how they think, feel, and live by committing to creative learning. And I've lived this transformation myself. So, if you've ever said, "I can't draw," "I'm not artistic," or "It's too late for me," it's time to let that story go. This chapter will prove otherwise—and better yet, it will show you how to get started.

WHERE DOES OUR CREATIVE INTEREST BEGIN?

What are the first musical notes we all hear in our lifetime? This is kind of a trick question, mostly because we all hear the same thing. The answer is—a drumbeat. It's your mom's heart beating, and as you lie in the womb and grow, you start developing a connection to music right off the bat! It's not rock 'n' roll, hip-hop, country, jazz, or anything else. It's a flat 1–2–3–4. So, when you see infants bouncing, tapping their feet, and shaking their hands and arms when they're literally three months old, that's because they are already feeling the vibe and they've felt it before. They've been to the dance club in mom's belly, and now they're ready to rock! It's undeniably true that everyone loves music, and, as we grow up, our preferences become more refined because there are specific sound wave patterns that connect uniquely with every person. And there's something for everyone; you see it in young folks, teenagers, young adults, those in middle age, and older adults.

When it comes to the visual arts, it is similar in that there is something for all of us. However, it's not as obvious compared to music. For most, our interest in making art starts when we're little, and we are drawing, doodling, and scribbling. It is undeniable that we love to do it, and it is one of the main methods of expressing ourselves in objective and abstract ways as young boys and girls. What also comes with being young is that we are also utterly nonjudgmental, and this contributes to our appreciation for art and reinforces our interest in doing it more frequently. But here's what happens: Our body chemistry gets in the way and interrupts things. As we start to grow, we thrive on being more active. In some cases, like me, we can't sit still at all, and this constant movement allows us to burn the excess energy that we produce. Along the way, when we are inactive, it becomes a lot harder to focus, and this conflicts with the stillness that is required to learn or make visual art. Music is way more portable, which makes it easier to enjoy as a passive listener and on the go. On the other hand, visual art requires a stationary commitment to doing it, sharing it, or absorbing it.

Notwithstanding the barriers that are involved with participating in visual art-making, from a sensory perspective, just like with music, our brains process visual art in ways that demonstrate strong natural connections and individualized preferences tied to form and color. But, no matter how you look at it, visual art remains deeply misunderstood, and I want to share some more about this.

If we look at our relationship with visual art throughout our lives, it presents an interesting storyline. When we were young, we all dabbled in making art at home, and most of us loved it. Then we took art classes in school, but quite often it was not the best experience. Most of the time it was also a low priority for our parents and the school districts. In fact, some of us never took another art class after middle school, and only a small percentage of us continued to take classes and make art at home during high school. Then, almost all of us stopped completely. Society told us that we had to get onto other urgent things: higher education, work, families, and all the other "priorities of life." In fact, most of us haven't taken a structured art class or enjoyed a compelling creative education experience in over thirty years!

All of this has contributed to the popular notion among adults that says, "I can't draw," or "I can't paint." But it's simply not true, and here is a weird concept to consider: For some strange reason, people can truly appreciate the time it takes to learn to play the piano, but they just expect to be able to draw or paint without any training or time commitment. Think about this. If you never studied music, and I asked you to play a song on the piano, you would immediately tell me that you have no idea how to do it and that you need lessons. But if I asked you to draw a flower and you struggled, why would you respond like most people and say, "I am terrible at drawing"? This logic simply doesn't make sense—drawing and playing music *both* require time for learning and practice. They both require an understanding of fundamentals and structural techniques. Here is the truth: **We can all draw, and we can all paint, and we can do them well!**

Why is this such an important part of the conversation around Growing or Folding? It is because my research and first-person observations over twenty years in leading creative education ventures confirm that for middle-aged folks, *art-making is a personal growth game changer on every level.*

> People who commit to consistent creative education and spend frequent time engaged in visual art-making are happier, more social, and better at dealing with change and managing stress because they are enhancing their brain development in the most compelling ways possible.

When you're doing it, you are *activating problem-solving skills*, and you are *thinking in new ways* that challenge your visual and fine motor skills at the same time. This gets your brain's neurons firing and *creates new connections that enhance your memory and overall sensory system*. And that's exactly what we need because, as we age, we eventually start to identify the complex challenges that we have been discussing. Holy shit, people—if you are not invested in your creative development, you are missing out!

> Art-making is a secret weapon in the battle to stay sharp!

You can pivot to building substantial new skills and capabilities, or you can choose to decline and be more vulnerable to neurodegenerative disease, emotional decline, cognitive decline, social decline, and reduced goal achievement. You can Grow, or you can Fold—need I say more?

So now that I lured you in by sharing the benefits of engaging with visual art, I want to expand on this topic because **the benefits that I've described are also attributed to almost every other area that involves putting your creative sensibility to work.**

That includes playing music, writing, woodworking, acting, crocheting, making jewelry . . . you name it. Creative growth doesn't happen by accident—it happens through the ways we engage in the process itself:

- Any way in which we challenge and apply ourselves to stretching our creative boundaries produces significant multifaceted growth.
- It works when we learn new techniques.
- It works when we are trialing solutions and experimenting.
- It works when we are reflecting on work in progress or our outcomes.

And most importantly, as discussed earlier, *there is an integrated relationship between creative growth, emotional growth, and functional growth that creates a multiplier effect*, and I have been exploring and documenting these outcomes for twenty years.

YOUR MOST VALUABLE ASSET: YOUR CREATIVE TOOLKIT

I have always been enamored with musicians, writers, and visual artists throughout my life. For a long time, I really thought that they were different than me. But as I grew and threw my life into the creative education space, I realized that it wasn't true. They simply spent their entire lives working at it, often supported with intense formal training, and they put their hearts and souls into their creative growth. They made it their profession of choice. In doing so, they developed a deep sense of confidence.

When I reflect on my youth, I remember an important moment in school that was not unique to me and had such a negative influence on how I approached art-making. I was the laughingstock in my seventh-grade art class. At thirteen years old, I had very poor fine motor skills and couldn't sit still, and this led to horrible outcomes and a realization: I couldn't draw a straight line! As a result, it led me to think, *I suck at art*, which also created a false notion that there was some score to keep.

This thinking carried over to my other creative endeavors where I became highly self-critical and routinely got in my own way. I remember starring in a play once, forgetting some of the dialogue, and thinking that I had no basis for ever acting again. Also, when I started taking guitar lessons at thirteen, I found it so frustrating when I didn't get it right away. But the truth is, I had no guidance in any of these endeavors and a mountain of negative teenage emotions to overcome.

This pattern of thinking led me to suspend all my creative activities in school. Having said that, today, I am quite confident that my creative toolkit is much greater than I ever thought it would be.

> That's because I learned to let go of the past, the self-criticism, and the unrealistic expectations that came with growing up.

Have you ever experienced a time frame when you were so overly critical of your creative outcomes that you just gave up? Threw in the towel? Stopped doing the hard work to grow?

NOW IT IS YOUR TIME TO GET STARTED.

There is so much power in trying new, creative things and challenging yourself to find the creative feeling that is sitting dormant inside your brain. I did this. And it was an organic process. But when I reflect on my life journey, I can now appreciate that I have truly devoted a good portion of my adult life to exploring a multitude of creative outlets, and this is at the heart of my health, success, and happiness. After my false start as a teenager, I applied myself and learned to play the guitar at forty years old. I even went the extra mile and wrote and recorded music, while pushing myself to perform my music live on stage! As a professional in the media business, I developed hundreds of promotional/advertising campaigns that stimulated my creative sensibility. Later, I stumbled on my interest in writing, and for the last twelve years, I have written a weekly blog for One River School called *Monday Thoughts*. And now I am an author!

I became consciously aware of the need to continue to invest in my creative growth, and I created a plan to challenge myself to do entirely new things. Recently, I took an improv class to tap into my childhood interest in acting. I love shooting and editing photography, and I am doing more of that. I have dug out some poetry and an old screenplay from the basement that I started writing in my thirties, and I am exploring this work with a fresh set of eyes and a new attitude. I am passionate about engaging in and collecting contemporary art, and I continue to curate art exhibitions. Lastly, I recently started making abstract drawings, and I can't tell you how good it feels to have come full circle and to have become someone who is fully practicing what I preach.

Consider these creative growth lessons that have supported my *pure growth*:

- I have pushed past the narrow boundaries of self-evaluation or the need to be great.
- I have learned to let my mind explore a broad range of what I can do creatively.
- This *playful* sensibility has added joy to my life and *allowed me to expand my mind.*
- I have become more connected to this other part of my brain that will serve me as I age.

Now, think about yourself:

- Do you challenge your own creative boundaries?
- Do you allow your mind to explore?
- Are you playful?
- Do you work to connect to your creative mind?

There is great power and growth in leaning into even one or two creative things that you want to try. It stimulates your mind like nothing else. I made a basic decision to grow by committing myself to **lifelong creative learning** a long time ago. I want to help you do the same.

Okay, here's a fun exercise that will get the juices flowing:

1. Get out a pencil and a piece of paper right now.
2. Don't turn the page!
3. I have a *two-minute exercise* for you, and you must play now.
4. Put the book down . . . go get paper and a pencil and come back. (I could already sense that you may have been ready to pivot away from this, and you must not!)

ONCE YOU ARE READY, TURN THE PAGE.

Here are two photos of iconic music personalities: Mick Jagger and Beyoncé.

Credit: Evening Standard / Stringer / Hulton Archive via Getty Images

Credit: Larry Busacca/PW / Contributor / WireImage via Getty Images

1. **Stare at these two pictures carefully.**
   - Check out their faces and expressions.
   - Think about what you are seeing and what makes them interesting and visually compelling.

2. **Select one of the two images to focus on.**

3. **Write five words that describe that person: e.g., *pretty, bold, evocative* . . . whatever comes to mind. Go!**
   - Here's a tip: Write whatever comes to your mind first and write fast.
   - Stop when you have five words.
   - Okay, now read the five out loud.

Now, here is your second exercise:

1. **Select the same image for a simple and fast *three-minute drawing*.**
   - Yes, we are going to scratch out a drawing of one of them in three minutes.
   - You must do this now or this book is worth nothing!

2. **Grab your pencil, prop the book page open, select one of them, and begin drawing.**
   - Let your arm and hand loosen up.
   - Work fast. Accuracy doesn't matter—expression does.
   - Creating YOUR work in YOUR way is what matters.
   - *Enjoy the experience and all the imperfection that may come with this.*
   - Go.
   - No judgment. Just draw!

Okay, let's review our workflow:

1. Read the five adjectives that describe the artist you selected out loud.
2. Turn the page and stare at your drawing.
3. What did this feel like?

For the last decade and a half, while operating One River School, I regularly taught a comprehensive management training program for new employees, and I designed this exercise within the context of group training on day one. This was where we talked about our company, our product, and our culture. One of the most critical points that I made was that it is my belief that we often lose sight of *the most crucial element of art-making*:

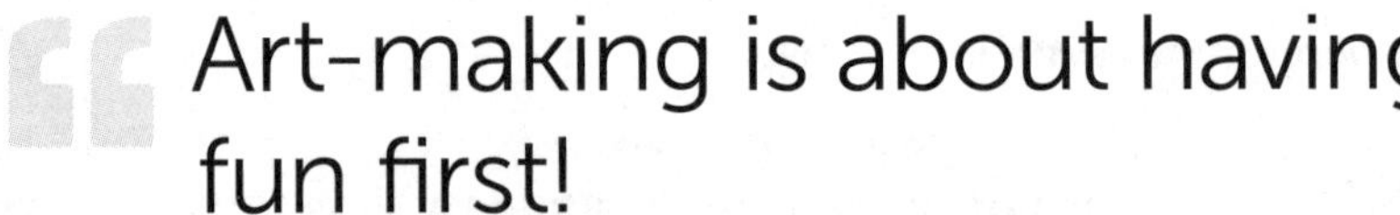

We all get stuck when we try new things, and we often struggle when we attempt new creative projects. But *surpassing the gap between that first feeling of frustration and your ability to loosen up and roll with it is the critical first step*. This is what is required to tap into the playful sense of wonder and joy that is essential to the experiences that help us grow, learn, overcome obstacles, and produce the right chemicals that reinforce the right feelings and emotions.

So, let's review. We did a basic written brainstorm to get loosened up, and then we tapped into the spatial side of our brain to complete a drawing exercise.

Here is the takeaway: **We are all creators.**

Our creative skills show up in everything we do as part of a continuum of natural creative talent that we are all blessed with, and it is dynamically influenced by the amount of time we put into it. But the *I can't*, *I suck*, *I don't* mentality is just not true. You have to get comfortable with the first step and let go, which allows you to invest in your creative growth and paves the way for expanding your horizons and improving how you think. This enhances your health, happiness, and productivity. I know it because I have been the beneficiary of watching thousands of students at School of Rock and One River School for over twenty years, as well as experiencing it myself firsthand.

THE ROSS CYCLE OF CREATIVE GROWTH AND DEVELOPMENT

Creative growth doesn't happen by accident.

It isn't magic, and it's not reserved for the lucky few.

I've come to understand that the people who experience the most transformation—those who reignite their spark, sharpen their minds, and build lasting emotional resilience—are the ones who commit themselves to a recurring, simple, powerful cycle of action/reward that keeps them moving forward.

It's not about talent. It's about momentum.

I call it the Ross Cycle of Creative Growth and Development, and it is a clear, repeatable loop that turns small creative efforts into massive personal returns.

Whether you're painting, writing, playing an instrument, or just experimenting with something creative and new, this framework explains *why* the process works, *how* growth builds upon itself, and *what* you can do to harness its full potential.

This isn't just a theory. It's lived experience—and it works. So, before you say, "I'm not creative," let's look at the real mechanics behind how your brain, your energy, and your sense of fulfillment begin to shift the moment you pick up the pencil, strum a chord, or try something new.

As discussed in chapter two, creative growth comes down to building blocks, and from everything I have seen and learned, there are a series of steps that drive it:

1. **Practice** leads to more **fun.**
2. More **fun** leads to **more time doing.**
3. **More time doing** leads to **improved skills.**
4. **Improved skills** lead to **better outcomes.**
5. **Better outcomes** lead to a feeling of **accomplishment.**
6. **Accomplishment creates joy** and motivates us to **practice.**

And this loop produces dynamic growth that stimulates health and happiness!

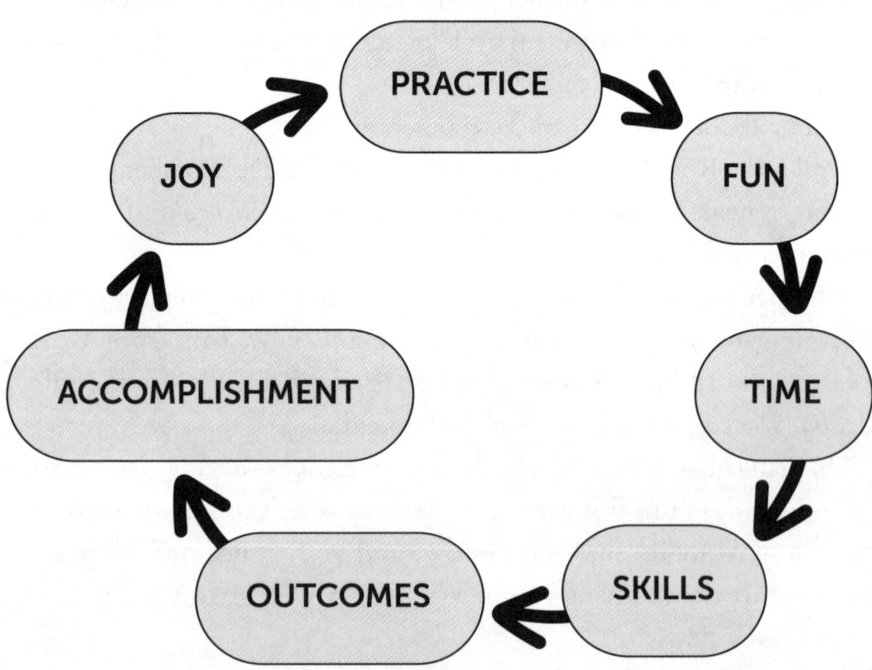

The **Ross Cycle of Creative Growth and Development** influences how you develop your creative muscle no matter the subject or medium—art, music, writing, etc. As you start to demonstrate creative growth, you start to feel personal growth. It influences how you think, act, and cope with stress and life's challenges. It influences how you solve problems and deal with simple and complex challenges. Your creative muscle works hand in hand with your emotional system to build coping skills and tools that are required for you to remain optimistic, and this is a key driver of health and happiness. It doesn't exempt you from all the things that we have discussed earlier in the book that are critical to your success, but it is an X factor toward strengthening your capacity to think, be patient, problem-solve, evaluate, trial new ideas, and prevent the erosion of these tools as you age.

SO WHAT IS YOUR NEXT STEP?

Putting **pure growth**—*functional, emotional, and creative*—to work for you is essential to refining your toolkit throughout middle age and beyond. When you deal with a personal crisis, you will possess the X factor you need to overcome the challenges at hand. Here's the truth: You don't need permission to create. You don't need a fancy degree, the perfect tools, or a childhood full of positive artistic experiences. All you need is the willingness to start—and to start *small.*

Creative growth is not a side note in the story of your life. It's the driving force that can sharpen your thinking, boost your resilience, deepen your emotional well-being, and help you navigate the messiness and beauty of being human. You've now seen how creativity connects with fun, skill-building, accomplishment, and joy. You've seen how it sparks a cycle of growth that impacts every dimension of your life. And maybe most importantly, you've seen how it's never too late to tap into that well of possibility within you.

So I challenge you: Pick something—anything—that lights a small creative spark inside you. Doodle in a notebook. Write a paragraph. Hum a melody. Take a photo. Build something with your hands. Don't wait until you "have time" or feel "ready." The act of doing is what makes you ready. This is your time. Not to be perfect. Not to be a master. But to *begin.*

Because when you do, you'll discover what I've learned through decades of teaching, learning, experimenting, and reinventing myself:

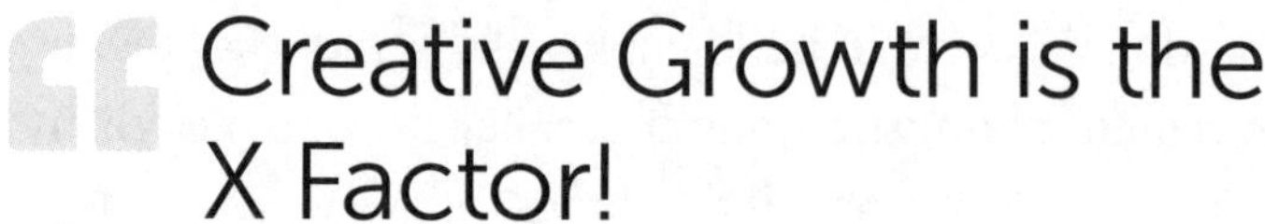

And once you find it, everything changes.

Let's go.

Scan QR code for the downloadable or digital version of the assignment:

CREATIVE GROWTH
The X factor

PART IV

THE WORK CONTINUES

If you've made it this far, you've witnessed the rawness of facing adversity head-on, the grit it takes to rebuild from the ground up, and the power of purposeful growth. But now comes the most important realization of all—the work never really ends.

Part four is not about tying a neat bow around the story. It's about what comes after the storm. It's about what happens when you've fought the battles, reached your goals, maybe even exceeded them—and then you wake up and ask, "What's next?" This section picks up in the aftermath of intense personal and global turbulence—grief, injury, uncertainty, a pandemic—and follows the process of recovery, reflection, and renewal.

In chapter fifteen, “A Decade Later: Clawing My Way through Life,” the narrative gets painfully real. We explore how physical pain, personal loss, and existential dread can converge and push us to the edge—only to discover that it’s at that very edge where we find our most resilient selves.

Then, in chapter sixteen, “Shifting Gears Near the End of Middle Age,” we see what it looks like to begin reclaiming joy. This chapter is about redefining success and easing into a different gear—not because we’re giving up the hustle, but because we’re choosing a more intentional, aligned way of living. Selling businesses, rethinking roles, healing physically and emotionally, and rebalancing life with a clearer sense of purpose—it’s the epitome of growth after growth.

Finally, chapter seventeen, “What’s Next . . . The Work Continues,” plants the flag for the road ahead. It’s a celebration of arrival—but not at the end of the road. Instead, it’s an invitation to live our next chapters with even greater clarity, curiosity, and compassion. What if the third act of life could be the most aspirational of all? What if the ultimate reward for decades of hard work is the freedom to reimagine what your time, energy, and gifts can do in the world?

This final section is both a culmination and a call to action. You’ve done the inventory, clarified your purpose, and embraced your pure growth. Now, it’s time to integrate all of that into a new lifestyle and legacy. The work continues.

CHAPTER FIFTEEN

A DECADE LATER

Clawing My Way through Life

At this point in the book, I bet you were expecting me to talk about how great things were one decade after turning fifty, after all the work I did. LOL. Brace yourself because new circumstances always lie just around the corner; that is the basic story of life.

It was the winter of 2022, and even though I had done so much to achieve my goals, it didn't matter one bit, because I was in agony and couldn't sleep, think straight, or focus on anything.

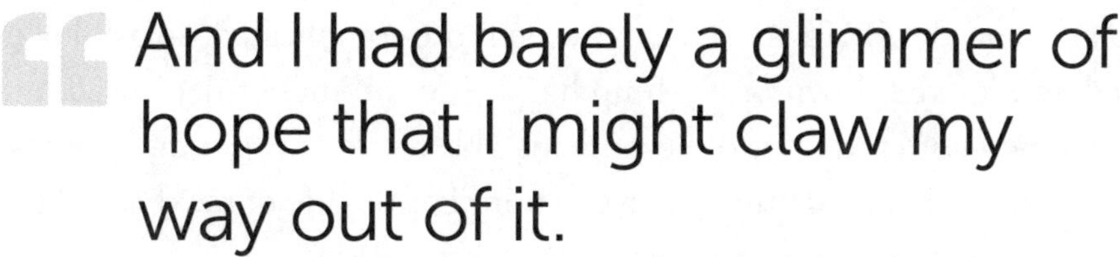

> And I had barely a glimmer of hope that I might claw my way out of it.

It was three o'clock in the morning on February 1, 2022, and I was on my fifth consecutive night of virtually no sleep. I looked down at my hand and wondered how the hell I got to this point. My left hand was paralyzed with three fingers fixed in a claw-like position. The technical term is *ulnar palsy*, and it was the result of a crushed ulnar nerve in my left elbow. To be more specific, I couldn't move the three outside fingers on my left hand, while my entire arm from the elbow down was pulsating in the most violent way possible.

The skin on my hand was both disfigured and discolored, the result of a flawed emergency elbow surgery and postsurgical therapeutic plan from two months earlier. Maybe worst of all, I now developed Stage 3 reflex sympathetic dystrophy (RSD), or complex regional pain syndrome (CRPS), which is a chronic condition that causes abnormal nerve activity and severe pain, and all of this was unlike anything I have ever experienced. I couldn't even touch the hair on my arm without jumping off the bed. No matter what I did, nothing seemed to offer any pain relief.

Every day that went by, I spent hours online reading research studies from the NIH and searching for anything I could find about my condition. There was simply no positive place to turn. All the muscles in my forearm, hand, and fingers were completely atrophied since they relied on the electrical impulses from my ulnar nerve that was almost severed. In addition, the research said that it would take eighteen months or more for the nerve to regenerate, and this freaked me out because the literature also said that if the nerve did not reinnervate the muscles within twelve months, I would lose all the function in my hand and fingers forever. I was staring at paralysis for the rest of my life with nowhere to turn. On top of that, the CRPS made things even more complicated, so as I lay in bed and looked down at my limp hand, I found myself depressed and consumed with thoughts of never being able to play my guitar, hit a golf ball, or even hold a damn fork ever again. For the life of me, I could not figure out how things could turn so dark so quickly.

Believe it or not, while all this was going on, my surgeon was advocating for me to do nothing. Literally nothing! He claimed that I needed to lie still and not aggravate the injured limb more. This plan, or lack of a plan, frustrated me beyond belief. My cousin David Feniger, who is an accomplished physical therapist, was in violent disagreement with my doctor's recommendation. David said that the clock was ticking, I was at risk for even greater complications, and the only way to treat this was to find a certified hand therapist and begin the long and arduous process of rehabilitating my injury. He convinced me to see an industry-leading hand surgeon named Dr. Keith Raskin in New York to get a second opinion on how to proceed.

I was a shell of myself when I walked into the examination room. I could tell that as soon as he looked at my hand, Dr. Raskin was deeply concerned. After a comprehensive exam and test, he put his arm on my shoulder and said to me, "I don't know why your doctor told you to do nothing. I trained him and this astounds me. The only thing to do is to begin therapy immediately and dig in for a long and consistent treatment plan. If it doesn't get better, we can transplant the tendons, and somehow, I can create some function for you." As I walked out of the examination room, I couldn't believe that two doctors could have two completely different recommendations on how to treat this injury, but it was clear to me that I was going to make my bet on this new recommendation and go to work on doing all I could to recover the function in my hand. The clock was ticking, and he was certain that I would see some improvement at the very least; while also telling me I would likely have to live with fingers that were curled no matter what.

Why am I sharing this story with you? To give you another personal and emotional illustration that hopefully drives home the most important fact of all:

THE WORK IS NEVER DONE.

Take a moment and ask yourself, Is there something in your life right now that feels stuck or broken? Are you listening to the voices that say, "Do nothing," or are you seeking out new information, new experts, and new paths forward? Just like I did, you might need to make a different bet on your recovery—physical, emotional, or otherwise. What action can you take *today* that creates inertia? Do you have a sounding board of trusted people to lean on? Are you taking advantage of the toolkit that I have shared to continually reassess and take inventory?

Did I mention that while I was now deep into this crisis, we were also deep in the throes of the COVID-19 pandemic and the previous two years may have been the most difficult experience the entire world had seen in my lifetime? Life was dark for all of us, and I wasn't spared one bit:

- I lost my mother in December 2020.
- I had to close the doors of One River School in March of that year and figure out how to keep the business alive with no revenue.
- Alex was quarantined from us with no capacity to understand what was happening.
- I was sad and stuck with the idea that Alex thought that we abandoned him.

This whole situation was in such contrast with all the successful work I had done to transform my life over the previous decade.

I had committed everything I had to improving my sense of who I was while clarifying what I wanted for the future. I built the best plan I could possibly build and started writing this book in 2018 because I was so proud of the work and momentum I had achieved. The book was now aligned with my purpose to help others, and I was excited to get things moving, to document my methods, and to share them with the world to make a difference. However, when COVID started in March 2020, I stopped writing and put the book in the drawer. And then, two years later, I was suffering from a freak injury and in the worst possible mental and physical place with no way to see past the storm that I was dealing with.

In April 2022, I was six months from surgery and three months into an agonizing therapeutic program. While working through a variety of exercises, I looked down and saw my pinky move for the first time in the most minimal way possible. I paused and thought that maybe it was a dream, but it wasn't. An electrical signal from the nerve fired from my elbow to my hand, and this slight movement in my finger triggered the most baseline sense of wonder and hope that I ever had. Maybe I wasn't paralyzed and I was on the precipice of seeing my dormant limb wake up!

I jumped up and called my therapist, Jayne, over to the table, and her ear-to-ear smile was such a beautiful reinforcement. She encouraged me to be patient and play the long game, and I committed to attending therapy two to three times a week until I plateaued. My goal, despite all that I heard, was 100 percent recovery, and I was never going to stop until I gave it everything I could. Before Jayne walked away, I lifted my clawed hand in the air and said, "When I can flip you the bird, I am outta here!" As I said that, I tried to playfully move my middle finger into position, but it was frozen and didn't move one bit. Nonetheless, I had taken a small step forward and now had extra motivation to dig in and grow.

A couple of days later my friend Dr. Marc Arginteanu, a retired neurosurgeon, came over to check up on me. Marc was guiding me through the medical uncertainty I was dealing with, but this was a seemingly different type of visit. Without any previous discussion, he handed me a book. I remember thinking, *I hope this is something that can help me with all the trauma I am dealing with.* The book, *Strength to Strength*, was written by the incredible Arthur Brooks.[8] When I started to read the jacket, I had a strange feeling inside because of the profound relevance the book had to the moment I was facing in my life. Just like the author, I was a striver who was working furiously on achievement for my entire adult life, and I was on a pathway to continue working that way for the rest of my life. Work had become a habit.

But Arthur Brooks suggested that we need to live the second half of our lives differently if we are to gain the profound joy that we deserve as we age. Wow. Here I was writing my own book that talked about transforming my life, and now this book was telling me that I needed to quickly pivot and refine how I spent my time to maximize the quality of my life. I owe a lot to Dr. Marc for sharing this book because it helped to kick-start a new window for me.

> I was now going to refocus on completing the cycle of goals that I set for myself at fifty years old, while also beginning for the first time to define how I wanted to live my life past middle age.

So I got out my pad and started to write. Here were some questions that I asked myself:

- Could I possibly be at a new and pivotal moment to transition to the next phase of my life?
- Could I get to the point where I wasn't working seventy hours a week as CEO of One River School?
- Could I move to a new role as Founder and become the "Chief Advocate" for the business, the team, the brand, and our purpose?
- Could I reset my financial plan to exit some investments and create more liquidity to enjoy my life differently?

- Could I change my habits and design a new plan with new goals that were unlike the goals that I've had for the last forty years of my adult life?
- Could I do all this and still be aligned with my purpose?

I want you to write down your own version of these questions. What are the roles, routines, or responsibilities you might be ready to rethink? If you could recall the ***my vison plan*** work we did earlier, this should look familiar to you. The fact is, in business we are always resetting our vision and goals, but most people never take the quiet time to thoughtfully think about and project the future that they want to achieve. You don't need all the answers right now—but clarity begins with curiosity. You may not be near the end of middle age, as I was getting closer to during that time, but it is useful at any time to thoughtfully express what your *second half* could look like if you chose to spend your time in ways that you thought would allow you the most abundance, joy, health, and happiness.

After reading *Strength to Strength*, I realized I could have everything I wanted for the future as I approached the end of midlife. While I was committed to overcoming the physical crisis that I was dealing with in the moment, I decided to recommit again to Growing and not Folding. I began to invest in every possible way to ensure that I figured out how to meet the moment. But to get to that place, I had to finish my work in the most critical areas that would allow me to transition past middle age.

First, I put a bear hug on One River School at the height of the pandemic to lead us through that minefield until the world normalized itself. Retrospectively, I was able to provide the leadership that my primarily younger workforce needed to get through the crisis, and, in many ways, I did some of the best work of my life guiding the team. The early part of the pandemic tested every business in America, but something different happened at One River. Our company came out of COVID way stronger than we were when we went into it. We refined our process and culture, and while we stopped opening new schools, the fifteen schools we built became a model for innovation in the art education space.

As we ended 2022, we were financially sound by refining our business into providing a world-class experience, and we started to build a new plan that was committed to scaling the business in the future. As the Founder and CEO of One River School, I had built a successful venture that was differentiated in the market, and now we had earned the well-deserved battle scars that proved we had the moxie and capacity to overcome adversity. In addition, I started to double down on my commitment to helping people grow and promoted my right-hand, Agnes Mauro, to Chief Operating Officer. My purpose, **to be positive and help people find their magic and creative inspiration**, was being met every day. This proved unbelievably rewarding as I fought my way through the myriad of other challenges.

In November 2019, Alex settled into a new residential program, only three months before the beginning of COVID. Reed Next, a division of Reed Autism Services, opened their first group home in Glen Rock, New Jersey, in December 2019, and Alex was invited to become one of their charter adult residents. We were absolutely thrilled to have him within twenty-five minutes of our home after seven years of living in Maryland and central New Jersey. Notwithstanding the fact that COVID created the most unpredictable scenario for an organization that was just beginning to provide residential services for disabled adults with autism, Reed's love, support, and commitment to the cause was undeniably clear. They were now a partner who was going to fight their way through the challenges of the world and assist us in fighting our way through caring for Alex. And as Reed stepped up, Susan and I continued to provide advocacy for Alex that got him through the crisis that was creating so many challenges for high-risk people with disabilities.

> How do I wrap my hands around the uncertainty of COVID and the simultaneous challenge of having my nonverbal adult son quarantined from us while living in a new place with new caregivers?

It was almost incomprehensible that we had fought so hard for so long to manage "all things Alex," but here we were dealing with another uncontrollable issue that was challenging our emotional state. Thankfully, as March moved to May, we were able to begin to take walks in the country with Alex and his team, and they were among the most special moments of my life.

> Meeting our boy at the beginning of a wooded trail and having his eyes lock with ours as he got out of his van was an experience beyond words.

Alex was safe! He was happy! He was cared for, and I started to be able to breathe again. Our man-child/baby boy impressed me again with his own immense perseverance. Finally, seeing him fight the fight lifted me up and motivated me to keep up the grind myself.

And during this window of time, Susan demonstrated the next level of love and oversight that without doubt will put her on the Mount Rushmore of moms one day!

While she will cringe when she reads what I just wrote, you must walk in my shoes to see the work she has done and continues to do on a daily and sometimes hourly basis to make sure the entire end-to-end plan that is in place to support Alex's needs get the attention it requires. It started the day he was born, and it will never end because of the pure and profound love she has for our special boy. She is built to do the work and hates to receive credit, but this is my moment to honor her in the best way I know how.

Our lifelong journey of advocating and caring for a severely autistic child is hard to understand unless you have seen it up close, in person, and at high frequency. Susan is so special and determined to stay in the trenches and give her heart and soul to him, and this was even more mission critical as the pandemic interrupted every aspect of normalcy in our lives.

As we were navigating through all the challenges we were facing with Alex, Susan and I were also trying to do whatever we could to help our youngest son. Jason is a thoughtful and kind young man who, like so many young adults, got thrown out of college in his final semester. This was supposed to be a well-earned moment, where one gets to party and celebrate the culmination of four years of hard work and growth, but when the doors closed for COVID, his college life came to a screeching halt.

Jason came home for spring break, and it turned out to be his final break. To make matters more complicated, Jason's girlfriend was living in California, and now he was quarantined from the world, living in our house, and miserable with us and with life. I had never had any disconnect with Jason; in fact, for his entire life, we had been as close as a father and son could be. Susan and I did everything we could to create a normal life for Jason and to make sure that he got all the love and care he needed while we tried to figure out how to deal with Alex. But now, for the first time, I saw a different side of him up close that made me deeply concerned. Jason was angry and not himself and deservedly so.

But the work Jason began to do on his own personal development had proven that he had the capacity to Grow and not Fold as well. In June 2021, he moved to Brooklyn with his girlfriend, Arianna, and shortly thereafter, he began to work, while continuing to commit himself to writing, recording, and playing music. His band, Moon Sand Land, became entrenched in the indie rock music scene, and Jason was doing all he could every day to improve his capacity to have the quality of life that he wanted. I watched him struggle, and I watched him persevere, and while this was happening, it also became abundantly clear to me that the growth that every member of his generation would gain by living through COVID was bound to make them better equipped to overcome future adversity and play the long game of life. Jason's task was to develop the motor, the muscle, the strategy, and the plan to maximize his pure potential. And my task was to be there to help as needed and to be the best dad I could be.

Every generation faces defining challenges. The real test isn't just survival—it's who we become through them. What muscle are *you* building right now that your future self will thank you for? Whether you're a parent, a leader, a friend, or just someone trying to do better—write down how you've grown through hardship. Then ask yourself, What's the next level of growth you're ready to reach?

AND THEN THERE WAS OPPIE

One of my best friends for over fifty years, Michael Oppenheim, lost his multiyear battle with small-cell lung cancer in April 2022. The ultimate mensch, Oppie had everything you could ever want in life, including an incredible wife, Tonya, and an amazing daughter, Sydney. Oppie also had many great friends and an unbelievably successful career as the business manager for some of the most exceptional music artists of our generation, including Jay-Z, Beyoncé, Eminem, AC/DC, and Kiss, just to name a few.

Oppie, who lived in Los Angeles, moved to New York temporarily during COVID to enter a chemotherapy trial at Memorial Sloan Kettering, and I watched him fight with every ounce of his being. Some days we would sit in his lobby with our masks on, or he would come to my house and get some respite in the woods. I will never forget the deep conversations we had as he fought with resilience and courage. I had never had the experience of seeing someone this close to me in real time go through such an unbearable struggle, which seemed to seesaw between improvement and decline on a steady basis. We became even closer during this window of time, and I was heartbroken when Oppie passed in April 2022. This was my first close friend to pass away, and given everything going on in the world and in my life, I just couldn't believe that he wouldn't be on the other end of the phone to talk to and share our life stories.

Oppie's death was a tragedy and another wake-up call for the precious and limited amount of time we all have to live our best lives. COVID disrupted everything; the whole world was in disarray, and everywhere I turned, people were dying, the sociopolitical fabric was shaking, and no one knew when things would stabilize.

Amid this backdrop, as I moved through 2022, I had a strange premonition:

> "I told myself to double down on my positive superpower.

And I started to lean in on the optimism that has always allowed me to move past fear and noise.

It is this optimism that has helped me push others through challenges and instill the confidence they need to see their way to the other side. I remember writing the following passage during the early COVID period and sharing it with family, friends, and employees to create perspective:

> During my six decades of life, every one of those decades brought us one or more massive challenges that we were able to endure: the Civil Rights era of the '60s, Vietnam in the '70s, double-digit inflation and unemployment in the '80s, the first Persian Gulf War in the '90s, 9/11 in the early 2000s, and the Great Recession of 2009-10. Every decade brings us one or more crises that create great concern, but the world always finds a way to rebalance itself!

So, if I was going to overcome my own personal crisis, I had to focus intensely on what I could control, and if I did so, I would be rewarded. When I reflected some more, I realized that I had met every challenge I had ever faced, so I started to dig into some new *growth tools* that would allow me to learn, adapt, and get stronger during this period. *Strength to Strength* set in motion the next level of work to crystallize where I wanted to get to, and another amazing book was helping me with new learnings that I believe can prove critical for your long-term well-being.

The Body Keeps the Score. Yes, it does. And it is also the name of one of the most important books I have ever read. *The Body Keeps the Score: Brain, Mind, and Body in the Healing of Trauma* by Bessel van der Kolk is a book that summarizes decades of research on trauma and its effects on the body and the brain. Every day that I was in pain, I worried about a lifetime of paralysis, and it was creating uncontrollable emotional challenges when combined with the uncertainty and tragedy that was all around me. But this book dove deeply into post-traumatic stress disorder, and it shed light on the brain's ability to change and adapt when recovering from trauma. Here is the specific and critical lesson from the book that may help you if you are fighting to overcome massive challenges.[9]

Question: When you study people who have the best outcomes after experiencing PTSD, what exactly did they do to achieve those outcomes? Said differently, if you are going to learn and grow from a traumatic experience, what do you need to do, and how can you derive functional and emotional growth from this experience?

The book told me that I should think about the experience I was going through, the work I was doing, and the long and challenging road that I was fighting my way through, and to **reflect on the positive lessons learned from the experience.**

That's because there is a reward system in the brain that says this:

1. Here's what I was faced with.
2. Here's the work I did.
3. Here are the results I generated.

So, if I could somehow find appreciation and learning in the struggle and journey that I was on, I could reposition the crisis and trauma into a mindset of success and achievement. In addition to carefully applying the book's main takeaways, I also learned how to facilitate healing through therapy and meditation, which ultimately promoted positive neural changes.

It fucking worked! As I became more conscious of applying this type of thinking to my daily journey, I started to turn from despair and worry to hope and appreciation. *And as my hand started to unfold* and begin to work marginally better over the course of the next six months, I was becoming better equipped to do everything I could to overcome my physical challenges while building a better mental bridge for the rest of my life.

The body keeps the score, and I was putting runs on the board and taking all the learnings with me.

It felt empowering as I continued to grind my way through my midlife transformation. I was reinvigorated, and now I was literally seeing nerve growth propelling my physical healing while the other aspects of my life were really picking up steam.

CHAPTER SIXTEEN

SHIFTING GEARS NEAR THE END OF MIDLIFE

Notwithstanding the physical and mental challenges I faced during the spring of 2022, there were some indicators that my broader plan was continuing to move me even closer to achieving some of my most important goals. Earlier in the year, I got a call from the CEO of School of Rock to see if I was interested in selling my franchise locations. However, I declined his offer. Selling the schools had never really crossed my mind because they were performing well, and I never imagined I would find a buyer to pay full value. In addition, I was so emotionally connected to my people and the brand because it continued to seamlessly reinforce my purpose every day.

But now that I had passed sixty years old, the idea of simplifying my life and letting go of some commitments was becoming a greater priority.

So, when he called again six months later, I knew that I would be able to negotiate an enhanced price for this transaction, and we wound up coming to terms on a deal to sell my School of Rock locations. Not only was I able to generate a phenomenal return on my personal investment, but all my partners were thrilled with the deal as well. What a moment!

All the way back in 2005 when I invested in and joined School of Rock as CEO, I threw my whole body into the business. I committed myself to simultaneously operating my own franchise locations, and our schools were consistently among the top-performing locations in the system.

We had not only built a great business, but young musicians in our communities also benefitted from the incredible commitment of some of the most amazing music professionals, people like Art and Jamie Lima. They were the Sonny and Cher of School of Rock, an incredible couple who devoted almost twenty years to building the business with me. They were my partners, and I was so gratified that they were going to participate financially in the sale of our business, which would allow them to make some critical life changes that they had been thinking about. In addition, Craig Sasson and Joey Cassata, two other extraordinary music educators, also benefitted from the exit. I couldn't be more proud and grateful to all of them for giving their heart and soul to the business. And, because of this transaction, I was now able to successfully answer one of the vital questions that I had recently asked myself:

> "Could I reset my financial plan to exit some investments, create more liquidity, and simplify my life?

I could now check that box!

GETTING INTO THE SWING OF THINGS

While the sale created a significant financial win, I was still overwhelmed and deeply concerned about my crippled hand and the potential for lifelong disability. But as time moved on, I became encouraged by some of the progress I was experiencing. I had been to therapy over seventy-five times during the previous six months, and I was starting to see some real positive changes in my hand that made me think that I might improve beyond everything I read or had been told by my doctors. As December 2022 approached, I had a planned a trip to Miami for the annual Art Basel/Art Fair Week and made the decision to bring my golf clubs to give it a go for the first time in over a year. My grip strength had improved from virtually zero to about 50 percent of full capacity. After a few days of basic chipping and putting, I went out on the golf course. I grabbed a club and hit some short shots, and I couldn't believe I had come so far from the paralysis that I had one year earlier. Jayne, my hand therapist, told me in the beginning that I wouldn't see the growth in real time and that "it would be like watching hair grow." But now, I was motivated to get outside and experience something physical. Trying to play golf would give me a new objective measure of growth that I could lean on to track my progress, and despite a year of trauma and hard work, my physical state was on the mend, and this contributed massively to my mental health and view of the future.

After two more trips to Florida in the winter of 2023, I set my sights on playing a real round of golf for the first time. I was able to hit the ball off the tee. Even though there was an overwhelming stinging pain, and I had trouble holding onto the club, I was happy to see the progress and be doing something I loved. I was still wearing a brace around the clock eighteen months after my surgery, but there were indicators that I was continuing to heal. I had now been to hand therapy over one hundred times, and the combination of a great team, hard work, determination, and luck was moving me in the right direction. I could now play a full round, and I was thrilled to be out there with my friends.

I decided to rejoin Knickerbocker Country Club in April 2023, and I signed up to play in the annual member-member golf tournament that took place around the end of May. Participating in this event was a goal for me and is always one of the highlights of the year. Despite the competitive spirit, such great camaraderie exists among all our members, and it would be a dream come true to compete again. My partner, John Masterson, was supportive, and even though my scores prior to the event were way above my historical level, he was committed to having fun and took all the pressure of the tournament off the table. Over the course of two days, we played in the most horrendous wind and rain. Even so, I played out of my mind. I was making crazy putts and doing all I could to help our team. It felt like Caddyshack! Somehow, John and I won our five-team flight and advanced to the final shootout event where we competed against ten other two-man teams to determine the champion.

Guess what happened next?

With over two hundred people crowded around the first green, the intensity level was high when John hit an extraordinary sand shot from fifty yards out. Since we alternated shots, I was left with a downhill six-foot putt to potentially win the tournament. After waiting for what felt like thirty minutes and doing all that I could to stay positive, I got up and hit a perfect putt into the back of the hole! Two more groups were left, and they both missed their short putts. We won the fucking tournament! Fifteen months earlier, my hand was paralyzed, and now my partner and I had beaten fifty other teams to win this important event!

It was an amazing experience and a full-circle moment of sorts. I was in a state of shock given everything I had been through, and it was truly a spiritual moment for me. How else could you explain that somehow, someway, I would not only have a chance to play golf again, but that I would also make the winning putt and win one of the most important tournaments of my life. That night when we received our awards, I got up to speak and was choked up. I was so proud, and to this day, I still don't believe it happened. This was a real change point for me.

> The body keeps the score and so does the golf scorecard!

The experience reinforced that all the hard work I had done was worth it. And it told me that I was going to continue to get physically stronger and maybe I could achieve 100 percent recovery. I couldn't wait to go back to therapy on Monday to share the results, hug my team, and push myself to continue to improve. *Overcoming this challenge in such a gratifying manner was perhaps one of the greatest achievements of my life.*

The emotional growth and confidence that I generated because of my success prepared me to solve two more critical questions at sixty-two years old:

- *Could I shift gears again and update* ***my vision plan*** *with new goals that were unlike the goals that I've had for the last ten years of my adult life?*
- *Could I do all this and still be aligned with my purpose?*

SHIFTING GEARS NEAR THE END OF MIDDLE AGE

On top of these fantastic turns of events, as the year progressed, One River School was on the mend, and we were able to emerge from the pandemic more successful than we were before the crisis. We worked hard from 2020 to 2023 to refine our consumer experiences and improve our team, and this led to us generating record results. Enrollment grew dramatically, and our summer camp program had now become recognized as "the most compelling creative camp" in the country.

We were maturing, and the company was beginning to act like a well-oiled business that had the potential to grow into a national venture with hundreds of locations. I was proud of the work I had done leading us through the COVID crisis, and as I looked at where I was in my life and thought more about my journey, *I started to think that this may be the time for the professional transition that I needed to move to the next stage of my life.*

Agnes Mauro, my COO, was flourishing in her new role, and I had a moment of clarity. Provided that all things continued to progress, by the end of 2024, I would step away from the CEO role and promote Agnes to the position. In doing so, I would be able to successfully answer two more questions that I had created for myself:

- *Could I get to the point where I wasn't working seventy hours a week as CEO of One River School?*
- *Could I move to a new role as Founder of One River and become the "Chief Advocate" for the business while continuing to mentor the leadership team to find their magic and oversee our vision and strategy?*

Double check! The answer to both was a resounding YES!

I was no longer fifty, and the journey to *transform my life in middle age* twelve years earlier was now in the past. I started to work on *my vision plan* with the same commitment I gave it when I was in crisis a decade earlier *to guide me into the future beyond middle age* so that I would be happy, healthy, and fulfilled while living my life through my purpose.

If you find yourself in your mid- to late fifties, you should start thinking about this evolution. If you are in your early sixties or older, then you need to get going now. Life is too precious to continue operating in the same fashion, focused on the same goals that have been driving you through midlife.

Our lives are broken into three distinct parts and here are some rules I want you to consider:

- The third part of our lives is the one where we can become less encumbered and finally have more control over our time.
- We can embrace all our life learnings about ourselves and the world to refine our purpose and principles.
- We can become more optimistic about aging as opposed to living in fear.
- We can invest in our *pure growth* to push the needle on our potential to stay as sharp as possible and manage our self-limiting thinking and behavior.

I did it and so can you.

I want to share a bit more of my journey and provide a real-world example to frame the work you are going to do. But before I do, I want you to think about this:

> The most precious and limited resource is time.

Now that I had more liquidity and was in a better financial position than ever before, I started to evolve my plan and add some new elements that I never had a chance to focus on. I needed to shift my mentality from long-term investments to a lifestyle that I wanted to experience. My *vision plan* for the next stage of my life needed to change now. Abundant travel was no longer going to be a dream; it was going to get programmed into my annual plan. Getting out of the cold for portions of the winter was a priority, and Susan was supportive of these massive shifts in how we would allocate our time.

Given the overwhelming challenge of raising Alex, combined with my rigorous career, I had only limited opportunities to see the world. This always bothered me, and it was in deep contrast with my abundant curiosity. Now I was going to prioritize traveling, and as the world opened after the pandemic, I was so ready to embrace it. Susan and I went to Italy in May 2023, and it was the trip of a lifetime. It was a dream come true to see Rome, the Vatican, Tuscany, Siena, and Florence. We never could have done this had we not created a first-rate plan to care for Alex, with a partner in Reed Autism Services who gave us the confidence and peace of mind to go overseas.

As 2023 unfolded, I had another surprise from School of Rock that I had hoped would happen for quite some time. They were interested in buying out my ownership stake in the company. As an early investor in School of Rock, I had led the rapid development of the company but also frustratingly watched the company struggle in the years following my departure. Still, I was always a believer in the long-term value of the brand, and under the direction of Rob Price, the company found its way and had grown into its skin. It now looked like I might be able to achieve a lucrative exit *eighteen years after I invested in the early-stage business.*

It was wild that my investment had been tied up that long; however, it was out of my control when we sold the majority interest to private equity. Now the firm was proposing a purchase of my stock, leading me to think the sale of the company and a larger return might be imminent. I decided to reject their offer, leading to multiple new offers, and I decided to pass on all of them. I had been so patient up until this point, and something told me that a more substantial sale and exit were in the cards for the company. Guess what? In August 2023, Sterling Partners sold the School of Rock to Roark Capital for a significant multiple, and my early partners and I received a lucrative exit. This was the elusive financial outcome that I had always hoped for, and now it was a reality. It felt like a dream.

While I had built an excellent financial plan with significant net worth, my goal of having financial abundance was something I knew would happen someday. I always believed in myself, and my strategic sensibility and perseverance were rewarded. Now I had to get focused on figuring out how to stay grounded through this experience. Susan and I already had everything we wanted. Still, this financial windfall certified my new professional goal to leave the CEO role at One River and switch to a Founder/Chairman position. It also allowed me to go deeper into reframing **my vision plan** through the lens of allocating my time in the most coordinated fashion for the balance of my life.

As a result of this transaction, I created a vehicle to support two causes near and dear to my heart: autism and the arts. I figured that I could lean on my purpose by providing financial support to organizations like Reed, the United Way, and others, so they could help kids and adults with autism get the care and individualized approach to growth that they needed. A whole generation of kids with autism was growing into adulthood, and I wanted to advocate for this collective group in the best ways that I could. Also, my passion for the arts allowed me to identify nonprofits that were doing amazing things in New York and New Jersey, and the spirit of giving helped me develop immense pride for what I had achieved in life.

I also continued to build my art collection, another way to support artists while investing in my creative growth. By the end of 2023, my collection had grown to over 350 objects and had become one of the more compelling collections of emerging contemporary art built over the last decade. I now owned artwork from almost 100 different artists, and many of them were still early in their careers, where the support of a patron was essential to their survival.

This moment also spearheaded another significant change that I hope you will appreciate: **I decided to finish writing my book!**

At the beginning of the COVID pandemic in 2020, I stopped writing this book because I was drained. For the first year or two, I had no sense of joy, and my focus was on saving my business and supporting my family, friends, and employees while dealing with the constant state of fear. Then I had the injury to my elbow and the paralysis in my hand, and I couldn't type.

But now I was reflecting on the incredible strides I had made on every level from late 2022 through the latter part of 2023, and it was clear that now was the time to jump back in and complete this project. In addition, my book was another fundamentally important way for me to help others: By bringing my story full circle, I could finish sharing my journey while providing deep and clear guidance to help others transform their life in middle age and beyond. And it was part of my creative growth plan as well.

So I decided to target 2024 as a bridge year to the future. Leaving my full-time job and completing my book would prepare me to launch a new plan focused on living my life through my purpose. I was excited to jump back into writing with a goal to publish my book in 2025/2026, but somehow, it was also a strange moment for me. I achieved and exceeded all my goals—it was a weird feeling. I felt so much pride and gratitude, but it was also different than ever before because, for the first time in my life, I wasn't immersed in conquering something new.

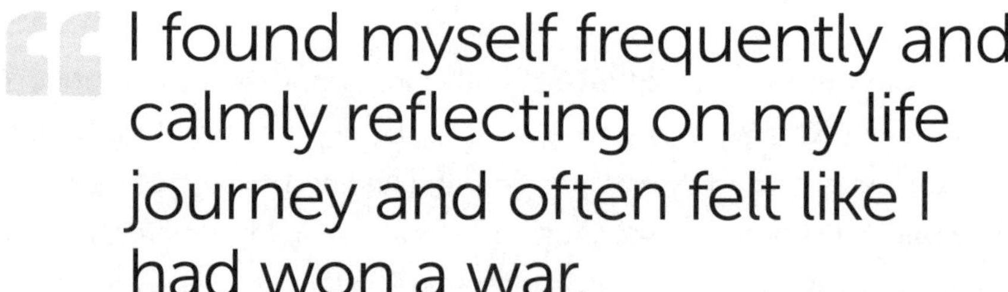
> I found myself frequently and calmly reflecting on my life journey and often felt like I had won a war.

It sounds a bit dramatic when I put it that way, but for the first time, I wasn't moving at the speed of light; I was reflecting on where I was and where I came from. I thought about the mountains I had climbed and the challenges I had faced, and documenting them in this book became a cathartic experience. While writing, there were numerous times I started to cry: when I thought about the precious moments, the challenges, the grind, the joy, and the journey of my life.

> Here I was, turning the page on forty years of work and sixty-plus years of life with the idea of resetting my vision, goals, and plan so I could live my most abundant life for the rest of my life!

My therapist, Ilana Rosenberg, provided constant support and guidance about thinking through this critical transition moment. It was about preparing my brain to meet the moment, to learn from all my life experiences so I would be better equipped to manage all the challenges I would face going forward. It took me back to the days of my son's diagnosis and near-death experience and to the days when my dad walked out the door, when I watched my mom decline into severe depression. And even though my brothers were continuing to struggle, I saw some improvements in them and I continued to work on optimizing my mental and physical health to do the best I could to help them, while not owning something that I didn't control.

As a result, I was now cured of the lifetime of guilt that I carried like heavy baggage.

I developed more discipline and a more structured sensibility toward doing the daily work, and I was proud of my stick-to-it-ness. My journey from the streets of Queens, New York, with little to no mentoring and guidance, to one of great success in business and life was now a solid part of my life story. And the fact that I have loving family and friends to share life with—wow!

GRATEFUL WITH A CAPITAL G!

The world rewarded my commitment to doing the work. I know I am not alone in this. That is, in fact, the way the world works. So, if you do the work, you should expect the world around you to conspire for your success.

If you have breezed through the work sessions in this book, don't sweat. Go back and work slowly through the segments to ensure you know where you are and where you want to get to. If you need help, identify a partner or friend in your network and work through this process together. The power of sharing these thoughts enhances the likelihood of you deploying the right plan and doing the work. And if you have already committed to the process, you must have the patience to play the long game, and you will be rewarded.

REMEMBER TO USE THE FREE TOOLS AT MATTROSS.COM

Scan QR code for downloadable or digital versions of all *Grow or Fold* assignments

If you were expecting a magical overnight transformation, forget it. I assure you that growth will occur by virtue of your intent and energy, so keep going and be clear about your expectations and the fact that there

will always be bumps in the road. Remember, my plan was going perfectly over many years, and then COVID, the death of friends and family, paralysis to my hand, and other factors punched me in the face again. But I never lost confidence that I would come out on the other side if I stayed committed. So stay motivated and use the workflow that I laid out for you to achieve your goals. This is required to transition your life over time. So be patient and be gentle to yourself.

THE JOURNEY AHEAD

As this chapter closes, I find myself not at the end of something but standing at the edge of something profoundly new. What began as a plan to transform myself in midlife has become a full-circle experience—one rooted in growth, guided by purpose, and made possible by perseverance. The story I've shared is not meant to be a victory lap, but a blueprint. It's evidence that reinvention is always possible, especially when you commit to the work, stay grounded in your values, and dare to evolve your goals as life shifts beneath your feet.

What I hope resonates most is that this process of change didn't happen in a vacuum. It happened because I learned how to ask better questions, how to listen more closely to my inner voice, and how to act with intention, even when circumstances were unclear or overwhelming. I learned to value emotional wellness as much as financial success. I discovered that healing is not only physical but also emotional, spiritual, and deeply personal. And I've come to understand that freedom in the later chapters of life doesn't come from stepping away but from stepping fully into who we are meant to become next.

It is inspiring to me that you have taken the time to understand my journey, and it's likely that something in my journey mirrors yours. Maybe you're seeking change. Perhaps you're building a new vision or recovering from a setback. Wherever you are, I encourage you to stay the course. Do the work. Trust the process. Reinvent yourself not because you have to, but because you can. It is a choice to Grow rather than Fold, and on the other side of that work is a life defined not just by what you've accomplished, but also by how purposefully you've chosen to live.

Let's turn the page together.

CHAPTER SEVENTEEN

WHAT'S NEXT...

The Work Continues

What if the question "What's next?" wasn't a burden but a blessing?

At this point in life, I've come to understand that asking that question is a privilege. It means I'm still dreaming, still growing, and still willing to evolve. Life, with all its twists and turns, surprises, and setbacks, has brought me here—to a place where I can look both backward with gratitude and forward with intention.

This chapter isn't just about reflection—it's about momentum. It's about honoring where you've been without letting it define where you're going. It's about crafting a new vision for your next chapter, whatever age or stage you're in. Whether you've just leaped, are standing at the edge of change, or simply seeking more alignment in your day-to-day, there's one truth I've learned that's worth sharing:

> The work never stops—but neither does the opportunity.

Within this final chapter, you get to participate in what may be the most compelling chance to think differently about where you are going long term. So let's lean into the most timely question I could ask:

WHAT'S NEXT?

It is a blessing to be able to ask "What's next?" and at my age, I have never been more profoundly aware of how short life is and how fleeting, rocky, and unpredictable it can be. So I am using this opportunity to step back and embrace where I've come from, where I am, and where I want to go next. This is the essence of trying to maximize our life journey. Life is about navigating a jagged road. But if you are grounded with a very clear vision for yourself and are focused on what matters most, chances are you will arrive at, or close to, your intended destination.

The lessons in this book provide you with another guidepost for continuing to create traction over time. When I reflect on my life, it is abundantly clear that I was blessed with a tremendous amount of natural capacity to stay focused on my overarching goals. I also had the resilience to fight my way through the bumps, and I'm grateful for these innate strengths. Having said that, I was prone to distraction and often chased the shiny object. When you learned about my journey and the complex struggles that I faced, I'm sure there were moments you could identify with and others that might have been foreign to you. No matter how you look at it, the architecture of our lives is the same; so if you want your life to continue to be aligned with your precious goals, make no mistake about it, **the work continues . . . always!**

As I sit here today, I reflect more than ever before and appreciate the effort that went into the last decade or more of my life. And, in October 2024, I am proud to say that I completed my professional transition by promoting Agnes Mauro to CEO of One River School. In the process, we adopted a new plan to grow our platform and transform art education dramatically. I am excited about the potential of this venture and its capacity to take the company where it needs to go on behalf of our extraordinary students and employees. With this significant change, I have checked off one of the most essential boxes in my life: leaving the CEO position while retaining the Founder role.

I have reset my schedule and have woven it to focus on being an essential resource to the leadership team, while also making sure I oversee the governance and financial management of the business. We are going to open One River Schools across the country and help more people of all ages tap into their creative interests. Along the way, I remain focused on my purpose *to be positive and to help people find their magic and their creative inspiration*. I couldn't be luckier given where we were when I started this concept twelve years ago. I chose to play the long game and said no to many short-term opportunities that I didn't feel we were ready to exploit. We invested in a team to evolve this concept, and now we can grow. At the same time, I have become completely comfortable with my new role and the chance to give part of my time to the greater good of One River School.

THE THREE LEGS OF MY STOOL ARE SOLID AS A ROCK

My professional goals are fully aligned with my purpose, and I now have some precious free time to add new personal goals in a way that excites me about tomorrow. This may be the most significant benefit I gained by making this professional transition a reality; my calendar is now heavily weighted with new personal goals focused on priorities central to my life.

I have worked for forty-two years with a driven sensibility, and while I have enjoyed it, it has also taken a piece of me. But now I can focus on doing things I never could before while spending more time with Susan and my friends, including traveling, hobbies, and sitting on my ass and doing nothing when I want to and not feeling guilty about it.

It didn't take long to fulfill my commitment to travel. But it came with a small sacrifice. While I wanted to start running and going like a banshee, Susan is much more deliberative and hates the process of packing and traveling too often. She is way better at being a homebody and staying in her lane, but we have agreed to carve out two international trips a year to see places that we've dreamed of seeing. As part of this, I decided to ask Susan to make a bucket list of places that she wanted to visit, and "all things Italy" was at the top of the list. After our first trip there in May 2023, there was a loud noise—Venice was calling! And now I was more than happy to travel there in 2024 because the city had just installed the Venice Biennale art fair.

When I got into planning our trip, I started to think more broadly and decided that we would begin in Vienna, Austria, which had always been on my bucket list, and then wind our way through Susan's motherland—her family's small-town village in the mountains of Croatia called Čepić. Her parents left this war-torn country in the 1940s and never returned, but now we could walk through its beautiful countryside and breathe in the air. It was such an incredible moment to visit places that seemed to be stuck in time, and her cousin Walter, who travels there every summer and stays in his parents' renovated home, invited us to spend three days with him and his lovely wife, Janet.

We had an expert tour guide through this enchanted place who provided all the history of the extended family over the last century or more. We even discovered Susan's mother's home, buried under trees and overgrowth, and after the first day of traveling all around the villages and the beautiful Adriatic coast, when we arrived back in Čepić, like magic, the most beautiful rainbow appeared in the sky, as if her parents were looking down on us from heaven. I was so moved by this moment and grateful to be with my wife on a broader journey that allowed us to drive through the lower Alps and navigate some of the most beautiful landscapes in the world. It was a dream come true for both of us to have the time, resources, energy, and motivation to experience this, and it reinforced my goal to travel as much as possible.

After our trip, Susan also realized that my motor wanted to go faster, and there were more things that we needed to get into right away. Bucket list, baby! I don't want to get on a SpaceX rocket, I just want to visit the spaces that inspire me. So, while we were talking about what's next, I decided to visit the Rock 'n' Roll Hall of Fame in Cleveland. This was long overdue for both of us, and in October, the Hall was hosting their annual induction ceremony. One of my dear friends Pam Kaufman is a board member and invited us to share the experience at her table. It was a magical weekend experiencing all things rock 'n' roll and getting to hang out with rock 'n' roll royalty.

Pam's husband, Scott Drath, one of my closest friends, is also one of my main music brothers. We have been to countless shows together, but this was such a special opportunity to share this moment with him as well. Scott was my former CFO at School of Rock and has been in the trenches with me through this entire journey. It just seemed appropriate that I had a chance to spend some time with him at this very important moment in my life. Scott continues to help me with financial oversight at One River School; he is one of the most solid people I know, and I couldn't be more grateful for his friendship. Perhaps the most challenging task of all was convincing Susan to get back on a plane shortly after our trip to Italy, but I got it done. My sales game remains powerful!

While I wasn't retired, I started to think that in some ways, *this felt like a mini retirement lap*. And why not? Isn't this what life's all about? All the sacrifices we make growing up, raising kids, and working our butts off need to be rewarded as we evolve and free up time. I have a new perspective about how I think about time—the most significant obstacle.

Every day, every week, every month, and every year is precious. It might sound formulaic, but when I think about everything I've been through, I am just left with a simple thought: **There is no time to waste.**

So I got the pass from Susan to extend my trip so I could hit the road myself and visit some important places and appreciate this once-in-a-lifetime moment. After Cleveland, I got in a car by myself, and my first stop was Ashland, Kentucky, to spend a couple of days with Art and Jamie Lima. After we sold our School of Rock franchises, they moved their family to Ashland, and it was a special moment to reconnect with them. I then leaned in on some solitude to slow my brain down, and I drove through the mountains of West Virginia by myself and hiked at some of our most beautiful national parks. This was a meditative moment and something I always thought about doing but could never act on.

My trip continued over the next week when I met one of my best friends from childhood Marc "Woody" Wasserman at the world-renowned Greenbrier Resort. The Greenbrier, located in White Sulphur Springs, West Virginia, has hosted almost every American president since it was built, in addition to being the venue for the Ryder Cup in 1979. The autumn foliage was perfect, the golf was terrific, and I had some one-on-one time with Woody, whom I love like a brother. It couldn't get better. Woody and I have been friends for fifty years, and he has been my most loyal friend over my lifetime. It was amazing that he would switch gears and meet me to share this moment.

Back to work? Hell fucking no!

I got on a plane the next month and went to Las Vegas to see my brother before heading to visit another amazing childhood friend Richard Clareman in Cabo San Lucas, Mexico. Woody and I spent five days as guests of Richard's at the most beautiful resort, playing golf, drinking tequila, exercising, eating good food, and sharing stories about our lives, where we've come from, and where we wanted to go. We all reflected on how much we missed our brother Oppie. Richard's generosity is unsurpassed, and I have such appreciation for him and his friendship. Next, I jumped on a plane and went to Los

Angeles, where I walked through the art galleries for two days, saw friends, visited museums, and bought some fantastic artwork.

Throughout my adult life, I have often heard people say, "I'm living my best life," and I would feel frustrated because it always felt like I was in the grind. At times, I was probably envious, watching them travel and enjoying what seemed to be a carefree life, without the burden of raising a disabled child. But I now feel entirely different about it. Back then I had no way of contemplating how I would align my professional and personal goals, but now I could take my foot off the gas on the professional side and press down harder on the personal side. That's what this transition at sixty-three years old has afforded me. It's a chance to become a new version of myself, and I am thankful.

> The work never stops on maximizing your health and your happiness!

So where do I go from here?

Well, where do we all go from here? Suppose you're sixty-three and healthy and motivated with lots of energy, curiosity, and financial capacity to do things you've always wanted to do. In that case, the only thing that could get in the way is not clarifying how to spend that time. So I continue to do what I preach every day, and I remain fortunate that I've put myself in a position to have a significant professional opportunity to keep me motivated on my terms, with personal goals and a purpose that will pull it all together.

> My three-legged stool is now built of iron!

A NEW SENSE OF CLARITY

One day, I was sitting around thinking that there must be a simple, one-sentence question to crystallize exactly how I needed to frame my life as I moved beyond middle age. And I nailed it:

> What's the most aspirational version of myself that I can live up to?

This simple but elegant question works for anybody going through this period of life. To get to this answer, guess what? I asked myself some more questions. (What a surprise ☺.) This list works well for everybody. If you spend time sorting through this with real intent, I assure you that you will dramatically improve the likelihood of maximizing your health and happiness. Ask yourself the following questions:

- How do I best utilize my time?
- Whom should I spend it with?
- What are the best ways for me to help people?
- How do I stimulate my creative growth?
- What organizations can I support?
- How can I maximize my time traveling and tapping into my curiosity?
- What do I need to do to optimize my healthspan and longevity?
- How can I make it all attainable?

Note: I also asked myself, What can I do to help One River School and the team build the most compelling art school in the world? And most importantly, for me to do it right, I needed to commit to one other key principle to stay above the twenty-four-seven madness that is part of our over-wired and angry world:

> Every day I need to maximize my optimism!

I used to think that my enthusiasm and joy were things I needed to hide, but now I am leaning into them at all times. It keeps me on purpose, and I have come to realize that it is a God-given superpower that fuels my joy, my love for life, and my commitment to helping others.

While some folks thrive on talking politics and macrolevel societal challenges, I go back to what Stephen Covey taught me, and I will say it again here: The most important thing you can do to maximize your happiness and well-being, is to "focus on the things that are of concern to you and the things that you can control."[10] If you are passionate about causes, then get involved in your local, state, or national government. I admire this because it aligns you with making a difference and not sitting on the sidelines, frustrated and angry. There are important causes in my life that I can influence, and I am committed to doing so, but every morning when I scroll the news, I have fewer answers and more concerns. In fact, today, I scrolled through fifteen stories in the *Wall Street Journal*, twenty-two stories in the *New York Times*, and fifteen more on *Fox News* and didn't read one because they were just regurgitating the same things that I've seen for the last week. Staying informed is one thing, but staying on task with what drives health and happiness is **the main thing**.

MY COMMITMENT TO YOUR GROWTH

One nuance I've learned about myself through writing this book is that I am convinced that I can help others and will devote my life to this cause.

It's not for money. It is simply who I am and what I love to do. In 2011, when I reflected on what I was good at and what I loved to do, it led me to create an art school that resulted in a blessing I couldn't possibly imagine at that time. Besides the fact that we have created thousands and thousands of exceptional experiences for our students and built a community of professionals who love what they do, I realized another important thing: I am an educator through and through. I was blessed with a keen sensibility around what makes people tick, and over my lifetime, I have been able to cobble together a platform that has allowed me to share it with others. Now, I must connect with everyone if I am going to be true to my purpose.

Earlier in the book, I shared the history of lifelong learning and the small percentage of people who take formal classes or commit to creative growth in their adult lives. It is an unbelievably low number, and it is impacting the quality of life for generations of people, with the potential to hurt society going forward. The research and literature tell me that neurodegenerative diseases are growing at a staggering rate. And when you combine this with the aging of our population, we are on the doorstep of a crisis that is abundantly clear. That's why I move forward and begin to assume a new role grounded in a straightforward statement: to make a difference in society by helping people pursue their dreams, improve their executive functioning, lower their stress, and maximize their happiness and health.

It is that simple. And it is abundantly clear: **Creative growth is the X factor.**

WHAT'S NEXT: THE MOST ASPIRATIONAL VERSION OF YOU

Now that you know what's next for me, what's next for you? We all know that the work continues, and it is my singular hope that this book has helped you better understand where you want to get to and what you need to do to get there. You spent time trying to better understand yourself, since self-awareness is a required component for building the right goals and plan. Along the way, you probably discovered some self-limiting behaviors that you will need to address. Whether you are forty, fifty, or sixty, I assure you that your ability to generate the success that you want is readily available to you, but it also requires you to have attainable goals and a real sensibility around what matters most for you. Don't compromise. If you have done the work of clarifying your purpose, then own it, because you will lower your stress, promote healthier habits, enhance social engagement, and improve your mental health. Studies also suggest that it can reduce inflammation and stimulate cardiovascular health. Need I say more?

It has been one of the greatest honors of my life to share this book and have you grow with me. If you read through this and haven't yet dug into the work, I am grateful that you were compelled to stay with me. In part one, I shared my story, including the mountain of challenges I faced in middle age, and within these chapters, I also provided my back story and established a baseline of ideas to help you think about the arc of our lives and the complexity and nuance that we all deal with in discovering who we are.

Part two allowed me to prescribe solutions to help you tackle your midlife issues. They were rooted in two basic themes that govern all success: identifying what's working versus not working and clarifying your vision to define enhanced success and happiness. We coalesced around the goal to reinforce your personal and professional lives while creating clarity around the critical theme of purpose. You can revisit this toolkit anytime and go back on your terms now and later to guide you through the ever-changing journey we all walk together.

Part three of the book was my commitment to helping you with your *pure growth*. It is indisputable that we all need to be focused on our functional, emotional, and creative growth to maximize our health and happiness. To drive your best outcomes, you must continue to grow: to get smarter, more flexible, more self-aware, more engaged, more thoughtful, more educated, and most of all, more creative.

Part four reinforced the most compelling fact of all: The work continues—always. Just when I thought I had conquered the mountain,

I fell off the mountain. From this experience, I realized that you must have great respect for the work that you do every day of your life to be happy and healthy. We are fundamentally here for a short window of time, and there is no straight line to success and happiness. It is a jagged one, but if you are thoughtful about how you climb the mountain, you will realize that the joy is actually in the climb and not ascending the peak.

What's next . . . is up to you.

You are the protagonist of your story, the architect of your future, and the steward of your time. This chapter—my chapter—is just one example of what happens when you align your actions with your purpose, your goals with your growth, and your time with what really matters.

Now it's your turn to go deeper. To build your own three-legged stool. To travel not just across cities or continents, but into the depths of your own potential. I hope you see now that reinvention isn't about abandoning who you were—it's about honoring it while still daring to become more.

And as you move forward, I hope you keep asking yourself the essential questions:

- Am I spending the right amount of time on the things that matter most?
- Am I surrounding myself with the people who lift me the most?
- Am I applying myself to the aspirations that truly inspire me and are aligned with my purpose?

Stay in touch with me at MattRoss.com and on social media so we can share our stories, and I can continue to reinforce the most essential elements for enhancing your growth.

This isn't a goodbye. It's a handoff. The tools are in your hands. The map is in your heart. And the next step is yours to take. Keep going. Keep growing. Keep becoming the most aspirational version of you. Because the work continues—and the best is still ahead.

REFERENCES

1 Covey, Stephen. *The 7 Habits of Highly Effective People*. New York: Free Press, 1989.

2 Covey, Stephen. *The 7 Habits of Highly Effective People*. New York: Free Press, 1989.

3 Covey, Stephen. *The 7 Habits of Highly Effective People*. New York: Free Press, 1989.

4 "CliftonStrengths," Gallup, accessed September 9, 2025, https://www.gallup.com/cliftonstrengths/en/home.aspx.

5 Covey, Stephen. *The 7 Habits of Highly Effective People*. New York: Free Press, 1989.

6 Covey, Stephen. *The 7 Habits of Highly Effective People*. New York: Free Press, 1989.

7 Frankl, Viktor. *Man's Search for Meaning*. Translated by Ilse Lasch. Boston: Beacon Press, 1959.

8 Brooks, Arthur. *From Strength to Strength: Finding Success, Happiness, and Deep Purpose in the Second Half of Life*. New York: Penguin, 2022.

9 Kolk, Bessel van der. *The Body Keeps the Score: Brain, Mind, and Body in the Healing of Trauma*. New York: Viking Press, 2014.

10 Covey, Stephen. *The 7 Habits of Highly Effective People*. New York: Free Press, 1989.

ACKNOWLEDGMENTS

Inspiration jumps out at you in strange ways. If you told me that one day I was going to build a music school or an art school, I would have said you were nuts. And, I probably would have said the same thing if you told me I was going to write a book! But, as you can see, I am a lifelong learner who has come to terms with a profound sense of purpose to help others, and this inspired me to tell my story and to share my acquired knowledge.

Truth be told, inspiration was first and foremost around me all the time in my wife, Susan. She is simply different: smart, caring, passionate, and loyal. At the time I finished writing this book in 2024, we celebrated thirty years together and I am grateful for everything she does and stands for. My son Alex has taught me more about life than anyone else; your greatest blessings are often tied together with your greatest challenges. We call him "the moon" and I am simply better because of him. And to my son Jason, who has been the most incredible blessing a father could ask for, I am eternally grateful for your kindness, love, compassion, and of course, your inspirationally creative brain that connected with mine from the time you were a young kid right through to this moment.

Special thanks go out to Justin Spizman, who took my manuscript and both carefully and thoughtfully helped me refine it into the book it is today. His time, commitment, and personal touch are deeply woven into the words you read. Thank you to the team at Amplify Publishing who believed in this story and have already taught me a lot about what it takes to produce a high-quality book and how to get it in front of people.

I want to recognize all the people I've worked with over the course of my career. While I've spent a significant amount of time leading teams, the truth is that every day I learned and grew because of the input I got from you and the collaborative experience that was almost always in play. I am deeply inquisitive, curious, and interested in people, and my professional experiences and relationships mean the world to me and have helped to inform the person I became and the learning that I've shared in this book.

To my current team at One River School, I am in awe of your passion for helping others tap into their creative sensibility. Building and operating an art school is not for the faint of heart. Much like running a restaurant, it's labor intensive and there's a million moving parts at all times to make sure our customers are well cared for and our students get what they need to maximize their experience. Special thanks to my CEO Agnes Mauro, Angela Shin, our VP of Operations, Erin Champion, our VP of Education, and Maeve Collins, our Special Assistant to the Leadership Team. In addition, thanks to Krista DeRuvo, who is putting her heart and soul every day into helping me share this story with communities around the country.

To the musicians and artists of the world, you continue to inspire me. From Allman to Zappa and everyone between, it is about making the work and presenting your voice in your own authentic way, and I've learned to tap into the artist in myself and allow my individuality to shine in writing this book. I have dabbled in so many creative endeavors and my efforts at both the School of Rock and One River School have reinforced every day for the last twenty years that Creative Growth is the X factor in life. Our creative sensibility is what makes us uniquely human, and I will continue to do what I can to support artists of all types and help more people tap into their creative inspiration.

Finally, to everyone who works to support people with autism across the world, you have a very special place in my heart, and I have the utmost respect for you. Quite often, you help to give a voice to people who literally have no voice, and provide comfort for people who can't advocate for themselves. There are so many causes out there, but we know firsthand what those special moments feel like when you have a breakthrough helping someone on the spectrum. Your commitment to the cause is something that I have often felt goes unnoticed and unrecognized, and I want to put you right here, front and center, to say thank you and to give you the greatest and most widespread appreciation I could possibly offer. I will continue to do everything I can to support your community.

ABOUT THE AUTHOR

Matt Ross is an entrepreneur, author, and media executive with nearly thirty years of experience building businesses that inspire passion and creativity. From rocking New York's airwaves to scaling global education brands, he's spent his career blending business savvy with a passion for the arts. Now, he is the author of *Grow or Fold*, a profound story of awakening your enthusiasm for growth with a call to action to transform yourself in midlife and beyond.

Since 2012, Matt has been the Founder and CEO of One River School, a company whose mission is to "Transform Art Education®." Today, One River School operates fifteen schools in six states with plans for substantial growth over the next five years. In 2005, Matt invested in and became the CEO of School of Rock and turned a struggling music education startup into a dominant brand. Under his leadership, the company grew from five to fifty-five locations, while securing commitments for another fifty locations. In 2009, he engineered a sale of majority ownership to Sterling Capital and stayed on as an investor and multi-unit franchise operator until its sale to Roark Capital in 2023.

From 1989 to 2005, Matt led some of the most important radio brands, including: Q104.3, New York's Classic Rock Station, and Hot 97, New York's Hip Hop Station. Matt was featured in *Crain's New York Business*'s "40 Under 40" and is responsible for increasing shareholder value by billions of dollars for Clear Channel, Viacom, Emmis, and Broadcasting Partners Inc.

Matt holds an MBA in Finance from the Stern School of Business at NYU and is a *cum laude* graduate in Marketing from SUNY Albany. He is also a former member of the Board of Trustees for Art 21 and the Bergen Performing Arts Center.

His advocacy efforts focus on two main areas: supporting organizations that build communities for adults with autism, such as Reed Autism Services and United Way of Bergen County, and championing artists and arts-based organizations. Along the way, he has also built a personal collection of contemporary art that now includes over 400 artworks from more than 100 artists.